C000302550

ART DECO TRAVE
A Guide to Australia & Nev

NORTHERN
TERRITORY

QUEENSLAND

NORTH
ISLAND

WESTERN
AUSTRALIA

SOUTH
AUSTRALIA

NEW
SOUTH
WALES

VICTORIA

SOUTH
ISLAND

TASMANIA

To Pamela & Susan

ART DECO TRAVELLER

A Guide to Australia & New Zealand

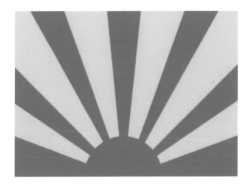

Edited by E. Riggs

Art Deco Publisher, 2020

Printed by Melita Press

Art Deco Publisher
Kemp House, 152 City Road, LONDON EC1V 2NX
artdeco-traveller.co.uk

Art Deco Traveller ®
Text Genista Davidson ©
This edition Art Deco Publisher ©

ISBN 978-0-9934146-2-6

The moral right of the author has been asserted

No part of this book may be reproduced in any form, by printing, photocopying,
or by any other means without the prior written consent of the Publisher.

Art Deco Traveller ®

CONTENTS

INTRODUCTION

Defining Art Deco is not always easy, over the years and to this day debates have ensued; however, one certainty is that many facets are involved with this unique architectural style and design.

As Art Deco crossed all genres and all boundaries, we see a profusion of interpretations. These buildings often incorporate the national identities of the Country or Territory, displayed in the bas-reliefs or patterned materials that adorn the facades. You can find bold skyscrapers in Sydney, the hallmark Interwar pubs dotted all over the Australian Territories and an entire Art Deco city in Napier, North Island, New Zealand.

This book does not profess in any way to include all hotels, monuments or places of interest in the Art Deco style in Australia or New Zealand, due partly to page constraints. However, it has a clear overview of the notable worthy contenders in the varied regions. Some areas may not be able to boast of many hotels in the Art Deco design; however, they do have other notable buildings from when this style of architecture was at its height.

Poetic licence has also prevailed, as some of the hotels may not be architecturally Art Deco, however, being from the period they possess the glamour and nostalgia associated so clearly with the era. I hope this guide will whet your appetite to further investigate the vast and diverse Art Deco architecture and design that is on offer for all to see in these glorious Countries. Your first port of call should always involve seeking out the specific Art Deco Society represented in the region and a list is included in the acknowledgments page, these are a brilliant source of information and collectively celebrate and champion the Heritage and Legacy of Art Deco.

Enjoy Your Art Deco Travels!

WESTERN AUSTRALIA

Capital City - Perth
State Bird - Black Swan
State Flower – Red-and-Green Kangaroo-Paw
Area Total - 976,790 square miles

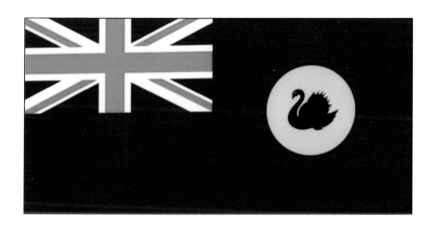

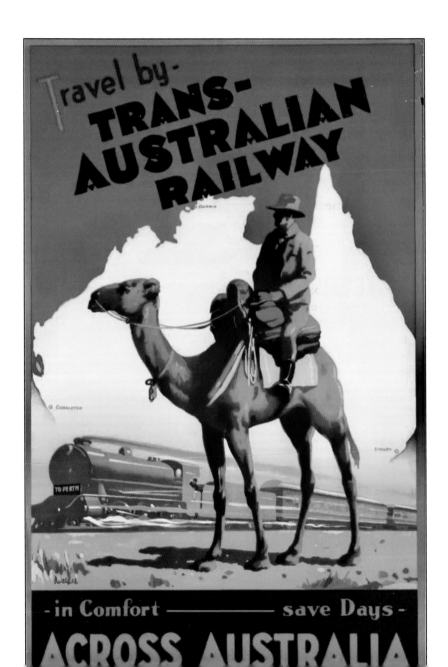

ACCOMMODATION

Criterion Hotel
560 Hay Street, Perth, WA 6000
1937 Hobbs, Forbes & Partners

There has been a hotel on this site since 1848 and it has been remodelled several times over the centuries and now sports its impressive Art Deco style façade and is one of the most impressive Art Deco buildings in the city centre. The new building cost $42000 and the furniture $7000 a huge outlay for the times in 1937. With its 69 guest rooms appealing to all budgets and its Mediterranean restaurant this is a conveniently located hotel as the main shops are within a 5-minute walk.

photograph © heritageperth.com.au

Carlton Hotel
248-260 Hay St, East Perth, WA 6004
1928 Eales & Cohen

This Spanish Mission style building a design popular during the interwar period dates from the late 1920's and has not lost any of its authenticity. It offers guest rooms mainly with shared facilities and is a well frequented pub and diner.

Hotel Beverley
137 Vincent St, Beverley, WA 6304

This quality hotel has 15 guest rooms that can cater for families with additional beds, for short- and long-term stays, these are nicely furnished in a vintage country style with deco touches. It has a restaurant with terrace a sports bar and games room. Overall, this is a great hotel and located near to Beverley.

Cottesloe Beach Hotel
104 Marine Parade, Cottesloe, WA 6011
1937 Hobbs, Forbes & Partners

A great advantage of this hotel is that it is located only a one-minute walk away from the beach. On offer are 13 guest rooms located over two floors and the double balcony rooms have a scenic view. With its three restaurants and the bar combined lounge means that plenty of good food and drink are available. The large Claremont quarter shopping centre is approximately 45 minutes away.

Sawyers Valley Tavern
10860 Great Eastern Highway, Sawyers Valley, WA 6074
1937 W.G. Bennett

This single storey restaurant/pub sits on the site of an old timber hotel. The resounding feature is the large Streamline central projection that rises from the parapet and rightfully this building is listed on the Heritage Register.

Perth City YHA
300 Wellington St, Perth, WA 6000
1939 Ochiltree & Hargrave

This former St Johns Ambulance building became Perth City YHA in the early 2000's after a large extension to the rear of the property and it offers 240 beds located in simple dorms and private guest rooms in a relaxed hostel. Facilities include a café, bar, and the bonus of an outdoor pool. The building is of considerable merit with its central decorated tower, set back wings, elongated windows, and speed lines.

OUT & ABOUT

Raffles Hotel
70-72 Canning Beach Rd, Applecross, WA 6153
1937 W.G. Bennett

This first-rate restaurant looks out over the river and is as impressive on the inside as the outside. The décor is glamorous throughout and nothing is better than dropping in for a cold beer or glass of wine. Unfortunately, it has no guest rooms.

Cygnet Cinema
16 Preston St, Como, Perth, WA 6152
1938 W. T. Leighton

This Heritage Registered purpose-built cinema has been in continual use since 1938 and is as popular as ever. The nautical theme is evident within the architectural style motifs, wavy lines and balconied tubular handrails along with oculus window features. The cinema was originally called the Como, however, it was renamed to the Cygnet in the 1960s to associate with the logo of Perth

which is the black swan. Over the decades alterations have taken place to accommodate modern technology, however, this is still a show stopper of a building.

The Moon
323 William St, Northbridge, WA 6003

This 1930 eatery has the bonus of being Streamline Moderne on the exterior and an authentic interior. Complete with its chrome speed lines adorning the walls and burgundy leather individual bench seats - this building ticks all the boxes.

Plaza Theatre & Arcade
650-658 Hay St, Perth, WA 6000
1937 W.G. Bennett

The former Plaza now known as Hoyts Plaza was the first purpose-designed Art Deco cinema in Perth having a notable symmetrical central tower which emphasised the prominent finial and signage. The original theatre had a seating capacity of over 1,200.

Piccadilly Theatre & Arcade
700-704 Hay St, Perth, WA 6000
1938 W. T. Leighton

When this cinema first opened on 10th March 1938 it had a seating capacity of 1100. The first films shown on the single screen starred Claudette Colbert in "I Met Him in Paris" & Charles Ruggles in "Turn Off the Moon". The building has suffered from neglect over the years, however, after part of the roof collapsed in 2017 the restorations programme ensued to save this important Heritage Listed site.

Regal Theatre
474 Hay St, Subiaco, WA 6008
1938 W.G. Bennett

This is a unique building with its circular tower, which is the building's most prominent feature conveniently located on a corner site. Therefore, it is the only cinema still standing in WA which opens onto a crossroads. The two-tiered half-cylindrical tower has horizontal and vertical detailing, with ribbed bands supporting the stepped signage holding the flashing neon sign.

Wembley Lifecare Physiotherapy (former Wembley Theatre and Gardens)
202 Cambridge St, Wembley, Perth, WA 6014
1937 F. Coote & S. Rosenthal

The former Wembley theatre was originally built of rendered brick and iron structure and had a distinctive curved facade. It also included

Chisolm House
32 Genesta Crescent, Dalkeith, Perth, WA
1930s Oswald Chisolm

This outstanding private residence was designed and built by the renowned architect Oswald Chisolm. It is a prime example of Streamline Moderne with its curvilinear balconied rooms and porch. The vertical stairwell tower with elongated slit window adds to the exciting aesthetic of this four-bedroom luxury home.

Claremont Medical Centre (former Highway Hotel/Coronado Hotel)
206 Stirling Highway, Claremont, WA 6009
1940 R. Summerhayes & M. Clifton

During its previous lives this building was the Highway hotel and is a prime example of Interwar Functionalist architecture that demonstrates the influence of William Dudok (Dutch modernist architect) on Australian architecture in the late 1930s. The wrought iron balustrade staircase was designed by Marshall Clifton. The building was renovated in 2000 and remains on the Register of Heritage Places of W.A.

Luna Leederville Cinema
155 Oxford Street, Leederville, WA 6007
1927 S.B. Rosenthal

The former New Oxford Theatre originally accommodated 1,286 guests and opened in March 1927. The debut programme included Vaudeville, music by the New Oxford Orchestra, comedy, and a special appearance by Miss Australia, Beryl Mills. It closed in 1968 and after several name changes it reopened in 1980 under its original name, until 1999 when it was purchased by the Luna Group of cinemas.

The two-storey facade is styled in Art Deco being embellished with stucco decoration, the original roofline has been raised and the veranda has been replaced. The side and rear facades are functionalist in character. With a full year-round programme of international and home-grown movies along with good facilities that include a bar, the Luna Leederville is well worth a visit.

Mount Lawley Bowling Club
Cnr. Strothes and Rookwood Streets, Mount Lawley, WA 6050
1936 W.G. Bennett

The Bowling Club was founded in 1909 and twelve years later in 1921 the 'Ladies Club' was formed. By 1923 membership had rapidly increased and another two greens and lighting were added. In 2000 extensive refurbishment of the original clubrooms was undertaken.

Nedlands Park Masonic Hall
6-8 Broadway, Nedlands, WA 6009
1935 W.G.Bennett

From 1935 to 2002 this impressive building served as the meeting place for the Freemason's University Lodge. It has a distinctive Egyptian Art Deco façade with traditional Masonic columns, and the internal Art Deco features. The two storied

© *The University of Western Australia Campus Management*

brick building has a tiled hall in the Interwar Art Deco style, an elaborate symmetrical façade featuring parapet with stepped skyline silhouette.

The entrance porch features terrazzo flooring and a foundation stone along with a recessed balcony on the first floor. The University of Western Australia campus acquired the building for a local enterprise hub for students and it reopened in 2018 after a full and extensive renovation and modernization programme.

Nedlands Tennis Club
Cnr. Bruce Street and Gallop Street, Nedlands, WA 6009
1937 Harold Krantz & Neil Perkins

Nedlands Tennis Club had its origins at the home of Mr G R Brown on the Esplanade opposite the Nedlands Park Hotel and in1938 a new club house was opened.

The architects were members of Nedlands Tennis Club and Harold Krantz's architecture was typically characterised by stark, clean lines with little or no ornamentation and this is a fine example.

Sir J.J. Talbot Hobbs Memorial
Supreme Court Gardens, Geoffrey Bolton Av, Perth, WA 6000
1940 Hobbs, Winning & Leighton

The memorial is seven metres high and represents a twice life-size cast bronze bust of Lieutenant-General Sir J. J. Talbot Hobbs, in military uniform.

The base of polished Mahogany Creek granite and the statue itself is mounted on a deeply fluted column of Donnybrook stone.

The architects in association with sculptor Edward Kohler entered the design competition to complete this and were awarded first place in 1940.

Premier Engineering were awarded the contract to make the statue and this was a first large project to be made in a local Western Australia foundry.

Attunga Flats
103 Thomas Street, Subiaco, WA 6008
1937 Marshall Clifton

The symmetry of the zig-zag pattern and six distinctive curved balconies make these residential flats an eye-catching feature of Thomas Street. It is believed that they have been owned by the same family since 1942. Retaining many of the original fittings, including doors, fireplaces, kitchens, and bathroom © *Perth Now* fixtures making these Interwar properties extremely desirable.

Bellevue Mansions
16 Bellevue Terrace, West Perth, WA 6005
c.1928 Samuel Rothenthal

Resembling architecture from Hollywood Hills these desirable apartments were originally built as two-storey residences. Desirably situated with Kings Park to the front aspect including views of the city and the Darling Ranges. In the 1940s Laurence Olivier and Vivien Leigh stayed here while performing with the Old Vic. Company which certainly put the building on the map.

Blue Waters
Canning Highway, Como, WA 6152
1954 K D'Alton

This centre piece house was built for Mabel and Keith Perron and designed at their request as a "Party Palace", becoming the hub of the Perth social scene for many years. It is primarily Art Deco with functionalist and cubist characteristics. The curved glass windows and frames could not be manufactured locally and were shipped from the U.K. The family were regular travellers and following a tour of Darwin, the Perrons' two young sons brought back two baby crocodiles, these were placed in a small pond in the rear garden! One was later donated to Perth Zoo after escaping from the property much to the neighbourhood's relief.

Kylemore
43 Jutland Parade, Dalkeith, WA 6009
1937 Horace Costello

This private house is a fine example of the Streamlined Moderne style, designed and built by Horace Costello. A novel and fun nautical effect is portrayed due to the cantilever balconies with steel balustrading coupled with the curved plate glass windows. It is a two-storey masonry and brick dwelling, with a hipped tile roof and projecting semi-circular bays to two sides. A veranda extends along the side and front of the first floor, with a metal balustrade, and the separate flat concrete roof is reinforced by thin circular support poles. It is well worth a drive past to admire this private residence. On many of my encounters the owners are only too happy to have admirers and are immensely proud of their homes, however, always bear in mind their privacy.

Lawson Apartments
2-4 Sherwood Court, Perth, WA 6000
1937 Hennessy (Hennessy & Co) & Reginald Summerhayes

Lawson Flats is an eleven-storey building and was said to be Perth's first block of flats. The building had a restaurant, shared laundry and caretaker's flat located on the ground floor.

The third to tenth floors were designed as residential flats - each boasting telephones, gas stoves, electric power points and a refrigerator. Each floor had a different colour scheme - either blue, green, or cream. Since its inception, the building has been utilised for residential purposes.

Mayfair Flats

83 Carr St, West Perth, WA 6005
1936 W.G. Bennett

This double storey rendered brick
building has a hipped tile roof, the
front façade is symmetrical above a
central entry point. The vertical bay
rises to a square parapet and has a
recessed window opening
containing a brick balcony and the
parapet has stylised lettering with
the name of the flats, all in all this is
extremely pleasing to the eye.

© *Realestate*

Perth has a plethora of other highly notable Art Deco – Interwar buildings and
here are a sample of many more of the delights for you to seek out: -

Mercedes College Music Rooms (formerly Rostrevor Flats)

173 Goderich St, Perth, WA 6000
1937 Cavanagh & Cavanagh

Featuring a curved corner, intricate sculpted geometric panels, the building was
given a conservation award in 1995 for its sensitive restructuring maintaining
internal structure and detailing.

Devon House

729 Hay St, Perth, WA 6000
1937 William Leighton

With a seven-metre-wide frontage, glass bricks from floors to ceilings, and clear-
glass steel-framed panels including the buildings name written in projecting
chromium letters on enamelled steel bars, this is certainly one to find!

Harper's Buildings
810-824 Hay St, Perth, WA 6000
1937 E. & R. Summerhayes

Home to the furniture firm, Maple & Co., a radio shop and the Break O' Day
Delicatessen. It was constructed in the Interwar Functionalist style of brick,
concrete, and iron. The building had a wine tasting room in the basement, and it
is decorated with 'Egyptian Terrazzo work'.

Motor House
68 Milligan St, Perth, WA 6000
1937 W.G. Bennett, Powell, Cameron & Chisholm

This three-storey triangular Interwar Functionalist style building with Art Deco
characteristics, is constructed of brick, concrete, and steel. The outer walls of
the building are rendered with white cement and these have been incised to look
like stonework. Three large openings onto Wellington Street allow vehicle
access to the ground floor.

P&O Building
56-58 William St, Perth, WA 6160
1930 Hobbs, Smith & Forbes

This building was considered unusual for the time using a steel-frame with outer
walls of concrete, concrete floors, and steel window frames, and the façade used
Donnybrook stone and Darling Range granite. The words 'Orient Line Building'
in bronze lettering adorn the parapet and a model of the S.S. Oriana, occupying
the main display window was continually on display.

Walsh's Building
88 William St, Perth, WA 6000
1923 Talbot Hobbs

The architect Hobbs is responsible for several buildings in the Perth Central
Business District. The building replaced the Economic Store that was destroyed

by fire in 1921. A food court was in the basement of the building, but this was extensively damaged by fire in 2007 and was forced to close.

First Church of Christ Scientist
264 St Georges Terrace, Perth, WA 6000
1939 Ochiltree & Hargrave

In 1926 the Church bought several outbuildings which were originally the Pensioner Barracks. In 1933 an auditorium was built as a temporary Church and the current building was constructed in 1939. It was finally dedicated in 1949 at which time the Church had become debt-free!

St Columba's Church
25 Forrest St, South Perth, WA 6151
1937 Edgar le Blond Henderson

Being a fine example of the Interwar Romanesque style, the building is located on the south foreshore of the Swan River. The significant features are the carved and coloured roof trusses plus the coloured leadlight glasswork.

St Mary's Anglican Church
9 Ridge St, WA 6151 South Perth
1936 W.G. Bennett

This building demonstrates a union of Gothic, Moderne and Art Deco architecture - this is especially noticeable in the foyer and articulated entrance hall. The windows were refurbished in 1970 signifying the addition of the colossal, monumental cross.

Perth Girls' School
2 Wellington St, East Perth, WA 6004
1936 AE (Paddy) Clare, Len Green & Len Walters

This stunning example of architecture incorporated the most up to date technology of the day – electronic clocks in all rooms and a broadcast system available in every classroom. The ground-breaking headmistress realised the importance of the radio as an educational tool.

King Edward Memorial Hospital
374 Bagot Rd, Subiaco, WA 6008

King Edward Memorial Hospital (KEMH) has been Western Australia's principal public maternity and gynecological hospital since 1916. It was named after Edward VII who died in 1910.

In the 1930s planning began on the Art Deco expansion to the hospital, which still forms the impressive main entrance to the hospital today. This was opened in 1939 and the architect responsible was A.E.Clare.

West Australian Ballet Company Centre
134 Whatley Crescent, Maylands, WA 6051
1937 A.E. Clare

This building was the former Royal West Australian Institute and Industrial School for the Blind. It was fully renovated for the West Australian Ballet company to move in during 2012. The state-of-the-art building now offers events and tuition for all levels of ballet in beautiful surroundings.

© *Western Australian Ballet Company*

Tivoli Theatre
Beach Road, Applecross, WA 6153
1934 Eales, Cohen & Fitzhardinge

This building is now a community hub available for hire and is known as the Applecross Hall. It was in the 1960s that the cinema closed due to diminishing guests, however, it is once again a hive of activity for the local residents.

Town of Claremont Council Office
308 Stirling Highway, Claremont, WA 6010
1935 Reginald Summerhayes

Claremont is home to approximately 10,000 residents and is 9kms from the City centre of Perth. The suburbs of Claremont and Swanbourne are home to large modern-day shopping centres and tree lined streets; however, you do not need to look far until you are confronted by architectural treasures like the Town Council Office.

Edith Dircksey Cowan Memorial
Kings Park, Perth, WA 6005
1934 Harold Boas

This monument stands at the entrance to Kings Park and pays tribute to Edith Cowan who was the first female member of the Australian Parliament.

It is also significant at it was the first civic monument erected to honour a woman in Australia.

©National Museum of Australia

Guildford Town Hall and Library
Corner James St and Meadow St, Guildford, WA 6055
1937 Eales, Cohen & Fitzhardinge

This structure has the presence and stature of an ecclesiastical building consisting of an exaggerated central tower that resembles a spire, and its oversized portico entrance. The building is making a serious statement of its importance. During previous decades it was utilised as a cinema and library, it now serves the community as an event centre and can be privately hired. It is National Trust listed and in overall good condition.

© Heritage Council Australia

Lord Forrest Olympic Pool
Cassidy and McDonald Streets, Kalgoorlie, WA 6430
1938 W.G. Bennett

Unfortunately, the original pool does not exist anymore, however, in August 2017, an official redevelopment programme was launched to restore and retain the existing Art Deco features of the site. In 1999 the complex was sold to the Goldfields Oasis Recreation Centre who transformed it into an amphitheatre. The new restoration programme has seen the former changing rooms become the shade shelters for the amphitheatre and restoration on the façade.

NORTHERN TERRITORY

Capital – Darwin
State Flower – Sturt's Desert Rose
State Bird – Wedge-tailed Eagle
Size – 548,640 square miles

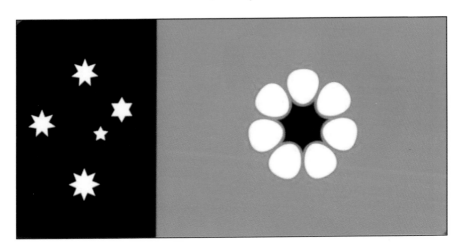

Much of Darwin was rebuilt after the devastating cyclone *Tracy* hit in 1974 causing mass destruction. However, the Northern Territory has some interesting architecture scattered around – of which a brief example is highlighted.

ACCOMMODATION

Todd Tavern
1 Todd St, Alice Springs, NT 0870

A relaxed vibe is what you will get in Alice Springs and especially at the Todd Tavern. This large corner pub offers good food and accommodation. You can choose from shared facilitates or go that little extra and indulge with an en-suite bathroom.

OUT & ABOUT

Rorkes Restaurant
22 Smith St, Darwin, NT 0800

Originally the Commonwealth Bank this building was constructed as part of the Federal Government's Civil and Defence Works Programme of the late 1930s. It is a rare example of early modern architecture in Darwin. It was completed in 1940 and the design included vents and overhangs to assist with climate control. It was sold in 2005 by the bank and now houses Rorkes Restaurant.

Burnett House
4 Burnett Pl, Larrakeyah, NT 0820
1938 B. Burnett

A trip to visit the only surviving house of the Government architect B.C.G. Burnett's Type 'K' design is well worth a visit, especially as this is a two-storey configuration. These houses were built to house the higher-ranking civil servants during the growth and development of Darwin in the 1930s. It is authentically furnished throughout and has an impressive terrazzo tiling feature. Th property was damaged during the 1974 cyclone and it remained vacant until the National Trust restored it in 1988. Guided tours are available and afternoon tea on certain weekends throughout the year.

St Mary' Cathedral
90 Smith St, Darwin City, NT 0800
Builder John Darcy

Outstanding in its design this structure earns it place firmly in this book. It was the Bishop John Patrick O'Lochlon who had the vision to design this large Cathedral and War Memorial and work began in 1958 and opening in 1962 (consecrated in 1972). It is dedicated as St Mary's Star of the Sea and visual references are abundant.

The design took elements of the architectural Heritage from the interwar period combining them with a contemporary Post Modernism twist to create something

incredibly special. It is a building that has tremendous energy and strength that radiates joy with its oversized ironwood entrance doors, stained-glass windows, and ethereal art collection.

© St Marys Cathedral Darwin

Aboriginal Madonna and Child by artist Karel Kupka

© St Marys Cathedral Darwin

Royal Flying Doctor Service Alice Springs Tourist Facility
8/10 Sturt Terrace, Alice Springs, NT 0870

The RFDS Alice Springs Medical base started life in 1939 and is now a comprehensive museum, using state of the art technology to portray the heroic lives of the Drs and staff who gave their services to the vast Australian territory. It is open daily and offers guided tours allowing you to step back in time, learn about the camaraderie and determination of these specialised people and the equipment and aircraft that allowed them to carry out their indispensable jobs.

SOUTH AUSTRALIA

Capital City – Adelaide
State Bird - Magpie (Piping Shrike)
State Flower – Sturt's Desert Pea
Total Area 379,725 square miles

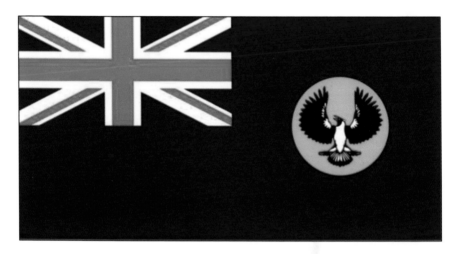

ACCOMMODATION

Mayfair Hotel
45 King William St, Adelaide, SA 5000

Opening in 2015 after a full renovation and restoration programme the former Colonial Mutual Life Heritage Listed building became the renowned Mayfair hotel infusing new life into one of Adelaide's ionic landmark buildings. It has 170 stylish guest rooms and suites, the Mayflower Restaurant, along with the Den Bistro, and the sophisticated rooftop Bar Hennessy on the 13th floor.

Renmark Hotel
Murray Ave, Renmark, SA 5341
1935

This building underwent several renovations prior to being extensively remodelled in 1935 in the Art Deco style. It is located on a long sweeping arch of the Murray River and is central to the town. The guest rooms are first rate, and you can choose from the standard which are highly satisfactory or select an upgraded room with balcony and extra mod cons. The bistro and outdoor swimming pool are also a welcome site and to top it all its good value for money.

OUT AND ABOUT

Hotel Bay View - Pub
11-13 Forsyth St, Whyalla, SA 5600
1941 Barrett, Glover & Pointer

This two-storey pub/restaurant is constructed of textured cement bricks, with cream and buff ceramic tiles at street level. Brick parapets face both street frontages, and corrugated metal sheet clad the hipped roof. Glass brick infill panels provide light to the foyers with doors of satin lacquered oak. The modern metal lettering in blue and cream enamel still survives on the upper level.

Piccadilly Cinema
181 O'Connell St, North Adelaide, SA 5006
1940 Evans, Bruer & Hall

This spectacular Heritage Listed cinema has distinctive chevron shaped windows. The architects worked in association with Guy Crick who was a renowned cinema architect. Originally it had one screen with a capacity to seat over 1,400 visitors, it was converted to three screens in the 1980s.

Capri Theatre
141 Goodwood Rd, Goodwood, SA 5034
1941 C. Smith

The Capri is a not-for-profit independent cinema run by local volunteers. It started life as the *New Goodwood Star Theatre* in 1941 and originally had seating capacity for nearly 1500 guests. Over the ensuing decades it changed hands on several occasions unfortunately losing much of its original Art Deco interior. In 1978 the Theatre Organ Society of Australia purchased the building and renamed it the Capri. They restored the building with local community and celebrity support and installed a unique Wurlitzer organ. A fully inclusive programme of events is available throughout the year.

The Regal Theatre
275 Kensington Rd, Kensington Park, SA 5068
1925 C. Smith

Located in a suburb of Adelaide the Regal theatre has had its fair share of name changes and renovations over the years.

In 2012 Republic theatres took over the running the theatre, it has the capacity for 580 guests and is a single screen cinema with a vibrant red velvet curtain. It gained Heritage status in 1983.

Former Hindmarsh Town Hall
Hindmarsh, Adelaide, SA 5007
1936 Chris A. Smith

In 1936 the building was a 2000 seat theatre accommodated on two levels, featuring a tiered gallery, curved ceiling and an arched proscenium.

The last screening was in 1966 although it was still used until it had a major fire in 1975. It is State Heritage listed.

Harbors Board
House, 2a McLaren Parade, Port Adelaide SA 5015,
1934-35 Chris Smith

This former official building has
been home to a Coca-Cola museum
and utilised for other business
purposes over the years. It
currently comprises of private
commercial premises. The exterior
of the building with its showstopper
entrance consists of concrete
layering to enhance its depth and
impact.

Former Brighton Council Chambers
388 Brighton Rd, Hove, Adelaide, SA 5259
1937 Chris Smith

This Streamline Moderne building housed the Brighton Town Hall and was the
former council chambers from 1937 until 1997. After the amalgamation of
authorities this Heritage Listed building became redundant and it is in the
process of being repurposed.

QUEENSLAND

Capital - Brisbane
State - Animal Koala
State flower - Cooktown Orchid
Total Area - 668,207 square miles

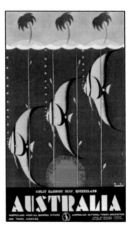

ACCOMMODATION

It is often claimed that Innisfail is the Art Deco capital of Australia. As Australia's wettest towns, Innisfail was hit by a devastating cyclone in 1918 and was rebuilt in the Interwar style. In 2006 a cyclone struck the town again and it sustained enormous damage, the town seized the opportunity to revitalize and preserve its existing heritage and multi-cultural influenced architecture. The varied styles of Art Deco incorporating Spanish, Sicilian, Moroccan and Italian facades are a wonderful sight to experience.

The Darling
1 Casino Dr, Broadbeach, QLD 4218

This new modern hotel has the high glamour, opulence and style that certainly bodes well with the jazz age. The modernist design of the building with its sensual curvature and the statement interiors with lavish chandeliers fixtures and fittings make it incredibly special. The luxurious 56 guest rooms cater for varying budgets and the added benefit of a top-notch restaurant and casino make this hotel a welcome decadent escape.

Prince of Wales Hotel
34 Main St, Proserpine, QLD 4800
Art Deco alterations in 1954 Cyril.C. Ruwald

For excellent value for money a couple of nights at the Prince of Wales is just the thing to discover the City en-route to other destinations. The standard of the guest rooms and shared bathroom facilities are particularly good. The restaurant and bar offer a hearty menu and like many of the pub/hotels in Australia billiards, darts and music entertainment are on tap.

Queens Hotel
74-78 Rankin St, Innisfail, QLD 4860
1926 Van Leeuween Brothers

It was two Dutch brothers who built this hotel opening in 1926. The restaurant has won awards for its good food and the large downstairs terrace is a joy to sit and people watch especially as the library across the road is Art Deco. The hotel offers several guest rooms with shared bathroom facilities. Approximately 60 miles from the hotel is the nearest airport of Cairns.

Australian Hotel
96/98 St Georges Terrace, St George, QLD 4487
1937

This hotel/motel offers rooms, some with River Balone views in the confines of a casual motel environment with the added bonus of a pool, restaurant and beer garden. Popular with tourists, work crews and military members transiting through.

North Gregory Hotel
67 Elderslie St, Winton, QLD 4735
1952 E.A. Hegvold

This popular hotel has something for everyone. It attracts couples, families, and singletons. All the upstairs rooms have balconies, and you can choose from standard or deluxe and all have private facilities. On site is the Daphne Mayo Dining Room,  Musical Fence Café, and the Horseshoe Bar along with the Banjo's Beer Garden.

ULTIQA Rothbury Hotel
301 Ann Street, Brisbane City, QLD 4000
1933 Hall & Phillips

Located in the heart of Brisbane this hotel gives easy access to all major attractions in the city. Luxury guest rooms and apartments are available in this 1930s building that was originally offices for the Shell Co. Facilities include a hot tub and roof terrace with BBQ area.

OUT AND ABOUT

Aloomba Hotel
27-29 Fixter Rd, Aloomba, QLD 4871

This pub has a welcoming façade and is a good old-fashioned watering hole. Do not expect any mod cons, however, a step back in time with a smile you will certainly receive.

Waterloo Hotel (Bar & Restaurant)
Ann St/Commercial Rd, Fortitude Valley, QLD 4006

This building constructed in 1937 is an upmarket bar and restaurant while still retaining a casual style. The outstanding streamline building is an iconic local landmark, and it has an impressive interior with modern and classical furnishings.

Cecil Hotel
42 Nerang St, Southport, QLD 4215

This 1930s bistro pub is a favourite with locals and visitors. It offers a good menu with a friendly service. It has event nights with stand-up comedy and a TV sports bar.

Coronet Flats
New Farm, Brunswick Street, QLD 4005
1933 Max Strickland

This three-storey building overlooks New Farm Park and features an angled foyer with wings that run parallel to the intersection roads.

The brick building also has angled bay windows designed to catch the breeze prevailing from the park area.

Empire Theatre
54-56 Neil St, Toowoomba City, QLD 4350

While this theatre dates to 1911 the significant Art Deco design was added in 1933 by architects Hall and Phillips. The interior is famous for its striking illumination of the grand proscenium arch with its constantly changing colours and decorative ceiling. It has the capacity to seat over 1,500 visitors and the Art Deco features have been fully renovated and restored along with further extensions and renovations over the recent decades. It is a highly prized events venue and has won many accolades over the years.

Gympie Fire Station
Bligh St & Nelson Rd, Gympie, QLD 4570
1940

Opening in 1940 this fire station which accommodates two fire engines also incorporates staff rooms, a board room on the ground floor, and the private quarters of the superintendent on the 2nd floor.

The watch tower was built to allow officers to keep a look out for fires. Superstition has it that the ghost roams the building, of a 20-year-old fire watcher who accidentally fell from the tower in 1943. Subsequently the tower was been added with a higher barrier.

McWhirters
Brunswick St & Wickham St, Fortitude Valley, QLD 4006
1931 Hall & Philips

This former department store is constructed of a steel frame with reinforced concrete walls and facework in brick and terracotta, situated on a truncated corner position it is richly decorated. The exterior facade of the 1931 building was designed to replicate that of the earlier 1912 and 1923 previous buildings.

Southport Town Hall
47 Nerang St, QLD 4215
1935 Hall & Phillips

This Heritage Listed town hall has seen many council meetings over the years and in the late 1950s and 60s rear extensions were added to the building. It has undergone renovation projects and in 2011 its original colour scheme from the 1930s was returned. If you happen to be visiting during the celebrated Open House scheme it is well worth securing a viewing of this beautifully preserved property.

Tattersalls Club
215 Queen St, Brisbane City, QLD 4000
1926 Hall & Prentice

Tattersalls is long associated with horse racing and this member club (that guests can also visit) has a stunning interior. The architects responsible for Brisbane's City Hall also designed this building. The Queen Street front was later acquired in 1935 and in the late 1990s further expansion and redevelopment took place. If the opportunity arises for lunch at this prestigious venue take it, also worth noting is that accommodation is available on the upper floors.

Archerfield Airport Administration Building
381 Beatty Rd, Archerfield, QLD 4108
1931

The Archerfield airport opened on the 1st April 1931 and has played its part in war and peace. The administrative building although designed in 1936 was not built until 1941. The airport is still used for civil aviation today. A Heritage Listed group of hangars is located at Kerry Rd, Archerfield Airport and these were constructed 1943-44 also by the Allied Works Council.

© *www.archerfieldairport.com.au*

Innisfail Shire Hall
70 Rankin St, Innisfail, QLD 4860
1938

This remarkable building was constructed to provide jobs as part of an employment relief scheme instigated by the Queensland Government during the great depression of the 1930's. It was constructed by Peter and William Van Leeuwin prolific builders in the town. It was severely damaged by Cyclone Larry and during its restoration project it was modernised keeping its Art Deco features. It has weekly free guided tours of the building and the dates can be found on the Queensland Shire Hall website.

© *Cassowary Coast Regional Council*

Fire Station
50 Fitzgerald Esplanade, Innisfail, QLD 4860
1937 R.Hill & A.J Taylor

In keeping with the other buildings in the town, the Fire Brigade was no exception to adopting the Interwar architectural style.

Innisfail Shops

Innisfail is known for its sugar cane and banana plantations; however, it can pleasingly boast an abundance of colourful Interwar buildings including the Innisfail Fire Station, shop facades and many more. This is due to a catastrophic cyclone that destroyed most of the town in 1918 and the result was to rebuild in the fashionable style of the period Art Deco. This takes many shapes and forms, influences of Spanish Mission, Functionalist, Frank Lloyd Wright and Art Deco harmoniously shout out as you walk around this interesting town. On the east side of the Johnstone River in Mourilyan Road at the top of a hill is the Innisfail

Water Tower that was constructed in 1933-34 from concrete and built by Van Leeuwen Bros. Be sure to seek out St Andrew's Presbyterian Memorial Church at 114 Rankin St, as the architect Eddie H. Oribin incorporated many of Lloyd Wright's elements to his award-winning design built in 1961.

Tait's Family Martial Arts Building
52 Fitzgerald Esplanade, Innisfail, QLD 4860
1940

The building was sadly involved in a fire during April 2020 and is awaiting to be restored most of the damage is internal and the exterior has thankfully remained intact. The two-story building is significant, it has a symmetrical façade displaying harmonious stepped features and ornamentation on the middle section above the parapet. The former Masonic lodge has an Art Deco wall and two large Corinthian columns with lamps, these have a special feature of shining light through the oculus stained glass window and a reflection of the words GOD appear within the hall on the ceiling. It was in 1926 that the plan to build the lodge was decided, however, this did not come to fruition until the later date of 1940 when it was erected. The building is now fully utilised as a Martial arts studio.

NEW SOUTH WALES

Capital City – Sydney
Territorial Bird – Kookaburra
Territorial Flower – Waratah
Area Total – 312 square miles

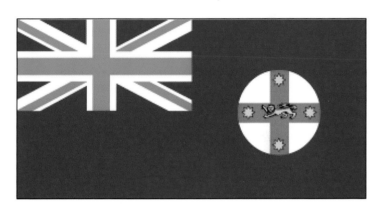

ACCOMMODATION

The Grace Hotel
77 York Street, Sydney, NSW 2000
1930 Morrow & Gordon

This listed National Heritage building was originally commissioned by the Grace Brothers as a showpiece for their successful retail business. The upper floors being the headquarters and the lower two floors as the retail department store.

The exterior is a majestic example of neo-gothic architecture which contrasts with the Art Deco interior that can be seen in the public areas.

It has **382** well-appointed guest rooms designed and furnished in contemporary modern, complete with a rooftop pool and bar, along with the Japanese restaurant. It is conveniently located in the centre of Sydney within walking distance to many of the cultural and social amenities.

Primus Hotel
339 Pitt Street, Sydney, NSW 2000
1939 H.E. Budden and Mackey

Opening at the end of 2015 this hotel was the former Sydney Water Board Headquarters, it has been sensitively repurposed. The exterior of the building was revered at the time and still is today for its precast features. These include using materials of marble, granite, bronze, brass, and terracotta.

It has 172 highly appointed guest rooms and suites with the overall interior feel of modernity, while incorporating Art Deco design in furnishings and fittings. It has a rooftop pool, bar, and restaurants all offering that touch of luxury associated with the Jazz age.

The original elements of the building can still be seen in all their glory and the hotel offers Heritage tours once a week to the public.

The Great Southern Hotel
717 George Street, Sydney, NSW 2000
1854-1930s

This Heritage Listed hotel has retained its original facade from the nineteenth century, however, a makeover in the 1930s accounts for its Art Deco interior of furnishings and fittings.

This includes a curved wooden reception area and bar, tiling, and light fittings. It has 167 guest rooms all with refrigerators and coffee/tea making facilities. It is located near to Central Station and Capitol Theatre and within walking distance of many other attractions.

Castlereagh Boutique Hotel
169 Castlereagh St, Sydney, NSW 2000

This refined and chic Heritage Listed hotel offers Art Deco style throughout. It has 83 comfortable and recently updated guest rooms at reasonable prices considering its location in the heart of Sydney near to all the popular attractions.

It has impressive dining areas, the Reagh Bar is hidden away in the lobby area and has cosy chairs where you can sip a cocktail with a light snack.

Progress up to level two and the Castlereagh Lounge offers dinner on certain evenings and breakfasts daily. The Cellos Grand dining room is located on level four and has an impressive, restored Art Deco interior.

The Australian Heritage Hotel
100 Cumberland St, The Rocks, NSW 2000

This historic Italianate style hotel that was partially renovated during the 1930s and is currently updating its accommodation and usually caters with single, double, and queen guest rooms mainly with shared facilities. The authentic Edwardian interior dates to 1914 making this building a significant Social and Cultural Heritage site.

Salisbury Hotel
118 Percival Road, Stanmore, NSW 2048
1935 H.E.Ross & Rowe

This newly renovated hotel and pub/restaurant has 20 guest rooms with shared bathrooms. A minimum stay of one-month is required, so if you are planning to use this as your base its great value for money and has a high standard of décor.

The Old Clare Hotel
1 Kensington St, Chippendale, Sydney, NSW 2008
1939 Sidney Warden

This hotel/pub was originally named *The County Clare* after its owner Margaret Maloney's birthplace in County Clare, Ireland. She bought the site in 1938 after the previous building was demolished to widen the road. She admired the architect Sidney Warden as he received much acclaim at the time for his project of *The Broadway hotel*, subsequently she hired him to design her hotel. Since a full renovation and restoration, the Clare building and the Carlton & United Breweries Administration building are one enterprise, and both are Heritage Listed buildings. It is refreshing to know that the hotel has kept with to its roots, the Clare Bar still has that razzmatazz feeling while maintaining a relaxed and casual atmosphere appealing to all. The 69 guest rooms are well designed and individually furnished, particularly nice are the Mary O' suite, Showroom suite and C.U.B. suite. To top it all off there is even a rooftop pool to cool off in.

Hydro Majestic Hotel
52-88 Great Western Hwy, Medlow Bath, NSW 2780

Situated above an escarpment in the Blue Mountains National Park this lavish up market hotel is made up of 16 buildings spanning over a kilometre.

The 67 guest rooms cater to various budgets and they are all arranged around the colour scheme of black and white to reflect its Art Deco Heritage. It was completed in 1904 by the retail magnet Mark Foy, and by 1920s and 30s, it was one of the most coveted places to be seen at. Heritage tours of the building are available at 11am daily for approx. $10 and include a full insight into the lavish Casino Lobby, Majestic Ballroom and Pavilion. In addition, there are seven restaurants and bars to choose from in opulent surroundings with an unsurpassed view. Perfection!

Mrs Banks Hotel
259 Oxford Street, Paddington, Sydney, NSW 2021

This Heritage Listed building dates from 1914 and it was formerly a bank building. It now houses an upmarket hotel pleasingly without the high price tags. It offers a high standard of modern-day comforts while retaining its historical features and feel. Particularly nice are the standard rooms with the glass cube window features. Located in the district of Paddington approximately 1.5 miles from the centre of Sydney this eclectic area offers many quirky cafes and bars.

Blues Point Hotel
116 Blues Point Rd, McMahons Point, North Shore Sydney, NSW 2060
1938-39 J.E & E.R Justelius and N.D Frederick

Located near to McMahons Point
Wharf ferry, the Blues Point offers a
good meal and fresh basic guest
rooms. Some of the rooms come
with en-suite and kitchenette and
these options are at very reasonable
prices.

East Sydney Hotel
Corner of Crown & Cathedral St, Woolloomooloo, NSW 2011

This traditional and
welcoming pub is known
as the last country pub in
the Sydney Metropolitan
area. It has been
historically restored with
open fireplaces, wooden
floors, and copper nails.

It offers six guest rooms
with shared bathroom
facilities at good value for
money. On Sundays live
Jazz is the order of the
day, what could be nicer
with a cold draught beer.

Alfred Hotel
51 Missenden Road, Camperdown, NSW 2050
1939

This pub/restaurant has eight guest rooms with shared facilities for either long- or short-term stays. The guest rooms are of a high standard and particularly special is the guestroom in the curvature of the building. Most of the emphasis is on the great pub, which also has a VIP lounge open until the wee hours of 4am. It is extremely popular with the locals and University students from nearby.

Knickerbocker Hotel
110 William St, Bathurst, NSW 2795
1939-40 R.B Fitzgerald
This hotel is conveniently located in the centre of the town close to all the amenities. It offers four en-suite rooms: - double, twin and triple, also a family suite. It has a high standard of service and offers a good menu.

The Gearin
1 Goldsmith Place, Katoomba, NSW, 2780

Scenically located in the centre of the Blue Mountains World Heritage Area, Hotel Gearin is a Heritage Listed building. It dates to the 1880's with the Art Deco additions from the 1920's. Its name derives from Mrs Gearin the owner in 1910. On offer are double, single, or family rooms at very reasonable prices. It is no longer a pub and solely concentrates on lodgings.

The Imperial Hotel
115 Murwillumbah St, Murwillumbah, NSW 2484
1931

This Spanish Mission building combined with Neo-Georgian architectural style was originally commissioned by Toohey's Brewery as a hotel.

After being beautifully restored it has many original features including copper pipes with functioning gauges hanging on the wall and concrete sinks from the 1930's laundries of Australian homes. It even has booths that have been made from the old bar and snug along with Chesterfield sofas in the games room. It really is a step back in time that maintains a light airy freshness. It has 27 guest rooms each with an en-suite and kitchenette

Clarendon Hotel
347 Hunter Street, Newcastle, NSW 2300
1934 Pitt & Merewether

Set in the centre of Newcastle the impressive Clarendon hotel, bar and restaurant has 20 stylish guest rooms. On offer are twin, double, and larger suites complete with balcony. Set in Art Deco surroundings the restaurant and bar offer a nostalgic and upbeat atmosphere with good food and service.

Bar Broadway – Longer Term Accommodation
2-6 Broadway, Chippendale, NSW 2008
1939 Rudder & Grout

Bar Broadway, formerly the Sutherlands hotel is popular with local students as it is near to the Colleges and offers good value food. It does have accommodation mainly concentrated on students in and around the area as a minimum two-week stay is required. However, if you are planning to stay a while it is well worth looking into as its great value for money.

The Erko Hotel
102 Erskineville Rd, Erskineville, NSW 2043

This great pub/restaurant comes equipped with a high standard of lodging.

The double, queen and family rooms have shared facilities, while the superior queen has its own en-suite.

It is conveniently located within a four-mile radius of many attractions.

Murwillumbah Hotel & Apartments
13 Wharf St, Murwillumbah, NSW 2484
1936

Located next to the Tweed River this comfortable small hotel offers single, double, and family rooms with shared bathroom facilities. Guests receive a discount at the adjoining restaurant and this budget priced accommodation is ideal to explore the scenic area.

Alpine Hotel
170 Sharp St, Cooma, NSW 2630
1938

The Alpine hotel dates to 1938 and has been fully restored. It has guest rooms accommodating all budgets ranging from executive suites to comfortable standard rooms. The 27 guest rooms are located over two floors and either are equipped with en-suite or shared bathrooms. The restaurant offers a full lunch and dinner menu, and regular evening entertainment and events are held in the bar. This is a great oasis to enjoy, ready for your outdoor adventures.

Castlereagh Hotel
79 Talbragar St, Dubbo, NSW 2830
1923

Built in 1923 this pub and hotel offers 24 basic guest rooms that are great value for money in an authentic setting. It has family, double, and single guest rooms and most have en-suite facilities. Complete with a spacious terrace and full menu on offer this is a great place to stopover and top marks must go for the original powder room!

Chelsea Park Bed & Breakfast
589 Moss Vale Rd, Burradoo, NSW 2576

Located in the Southern Highlands of NSW this exclusive house was designed by Ethel Noreen Garry a talented 1920s pottery and furniture artist. She branched out into architecture and designed several notable Art Deco houses. This property is located on the prestigious Chelsea Park area and is an upmarket B&B offering a unique experience.

From the minute you arrive be prepared to be transported back to the heady Art Deco days with a very warm welcome from your hosts. The interior is just as impressive as on offer are three luxury guest rooms. The Mayfair room with its lovely view over the front garden and access to the veranda has a 1920s-day bed and prize-winning furniture made in 1936. The Chelsea room is decorated in cream and pale green with a glamorous Hollywood style dressing table and a king-size bed that can convert to twins. The third equally grand guestroom is the Shibumi room that is Japanese inspired in its furniture and pictures.

OUT & ABOUT

The term 'Hotel' in the Out & About section is often a misdemeanour. Many of the once small hotels/motels/lodgings are now a bar and eatery without the capacity to offer overnight stays, however, they keep up the original name. Occasionally these establishments have a room or two that they still offer guests, however, these are not always overtly advertised. Also bear in mind that when a guest room is available, they most likely have shared facilities, however, it's always worth enquiring.

The Henson
91 Illawarra Rd, Marrickville, Sydney, NSW 2204
1935 Sidney Warden

This pub was originally established in the 1860s and was updated during 1935 and proudly displays its Interwar functionalist features. The exterior has impressive uniform bas-reliefs and patterned façade. It has an extensive menu including a good vegan selection.

The Unicorn Hotel
106 Oxford St, Paddington, NSW 2021

This pub/restaurant has a nicely presented authentic interior. The wood panelling, large painted map of Australia, green tiled bar and Art Deco stair railings all add to a great vibe. It has a programme of regular musical events and serves great food.

Hollywood Hotel
2 Foster St, Surry Hills, NSW 2010
1942 John M. Hellyer

This pub/bistro is a local crowd pleaser, and it offers a lively entertainment scene throughout the week. It is conveniently located a 2-minute walk from the *Golden Age Cinema* (in the old screening room of the Heritage Listed Paramount Pictures Building) making it convenient for a post or pre cinema stop. It gained its name from the connection to the cinema screening room.

The Golden Sheaf
429 New S Head Rd, Double Bay, NSW 2026
1936 Provost & Ruwald

This impressive pub/gourmet restaurant is the perfect stop when exploring Double Bay on the eastern suburbs of Sydney, a short ferry ride away around the bay. Facilities include a balcony, large lounge area and al fresco dining under the historic oak tree. If you approach via the back entrance in Kiaora Lane, a wall of fame is dedicated to the history of the Davis Cup in Double Bay.

The Golden Sheaf is located on the site of the old tennis grounds, and it was in 1909 and 1919 the Australasian Championships (now the Australian Open) and the International Lawn Tennis Challenge (now the Davis Cup) witnessed the Australian Gerald Patterson win the finals.

West Ryde Hotel
1021 Victoria Road, West Ryde, NSW 2114

West Ryde hotel despite its name is now a pub and cocktail bar with no lodgings.

The Art Deco facade has lost some of its former glory from renovations over the years, however, it can still be recognised as an Interwar building with much appeal.

It also has the added bonus of a quiet reading room area and a nice airy terrace.

The Imperial Erskineville
35 Erskineville Rd, Erskineville, NSW 2043
1940 Virgil D. Cizzio

This vibrant LGBT pub/bar and restaurant is home to top class drag and cabaret shows. It has an impressive cocktail lounge and terrace where you can enjoy your favourite tipple, whether that be the 1788 or the Pavlova whilst having a glamourous evening out.

The Hotel Marlborough
145 King Street, Newtown, NSW 2042
1940 John M. Hellyer

This pub is known locally as *The Marley's*, it offers good food, and entertainment in a relaxed atmosphere. The exterior of the building incorporates all the features that we associate with the interwar period.

Botany View Hotel
597 King St, Newtown, NSW 2042

This iconic designed building is a pub and restaurant and is well popularised and maintained. It serves good hearty meals in a showstopper building. Unfortunately, no guest rooms - once again do not be fooled by the word hotel!

Canterbury Hotel
208 Canterbury Rd, Canterbury, NSW 2193
1941 C. C. Ruwald

This casual relaxed pub and diner has event listings throughout the year. It serves hearty food and a good pint.

The iconic design of this building is one which will be replicated throughout Australia, incorporating sweeping Streamline Moderne features complete with curvilinear balcony and pillared entrance.

The Eastwood Hotel (Bar/Venue)
115 Rowe Street, Eastwood, Ryde, NSW 2122
1939 Rudder & Grout

Rightfully listed on the RAIA Register of significant 20th century buildings the Eastwood was purchased in 2007 by the Iris Hotel Group for $35 million.

Several plans have been submitted to renovate and re-open it as a hotel, so watch this space, in the meantime it serves great food and drink in wonderful surroundings.

North Annandale Hotel
105 Johnston St, Annandale, NSW 2038

This comfortable pub/restaurant has a large garden and kids play area and can cater for groups and functions. The spacious interior includes a lounge area with comfy armchairs to sink into, especially welcome after a long day sightseeing.

The Kiribilli Hotel
35-37 Broughton St, Milsons Point, NSW 2061

This 1937 constructed pub/restaurant is located on the north shore footsteps of the Sydney Harbour Bridge.

Particularly nice is the wooden panelled bar, complementing the overall design of the building. It has multiple bar and dining areas including a sports bar and terrace.

The Friend in Hand Hotel
58 Cowper St, Glebe, NSW 2037

This quirky pub/bistro once visited is never forgotten. It has an interesting array of vintage signs and memorabilia on the walls and hanging from the ceiling. However, it is the entertaining and happy cockatoo that also adds to its entertainment value. It also offers monthly events along with its good value for money food in museum style surroundings.

Golden Barley Hotel
165-169 Edgeware Rd, Enmore, NSW 2042

This friendly pub/restaurant offers an extensive menu in comfortable surroundings.

Like many of the pubs from this era you have the choice of areas to drink or dine in and this often includes an outside terrace like the one here at the Golden Barley. With a comfortable lounge and informal table and chairs all topped off with monthly music events and facilities for functions this venue encapsulates the essence of the Australian Interwar pub.

The Royal Sheaf Hotel
231 Burwood Road, Burwood, NSW 2134

Particularly nice about this pub is its authenticity both outside and in. The interior circular space is furnished in fetching green and chrome that compliments the Streamline Moderne exterior. Like most of these Interwar pubs the food and beer are great value for money.

Petersham Inn
386 Parramatta Rd, Petersham, NSW 2049
1938 J. E. Justelius

This building makes quite a statement with its red brick and central column contrasting with a white convoluted spandrel and bas-reliefs adorning the façade. It is a sports bar that serves food and on a Thursday to Saturday it doubles as a strip club.

Central Hotel
1 Napier St, Deniliquin, NSW 2710

You certainly cannot miss your approach to this hotel as it is a showcase of Streamline Moderne architecture complete with speed lines, vertical protruding spandrels, canopied balconies, and the token porthole window. Needless to say, it serves a good hearty meal, that's if you can pull yourself away from admiring its exterior.

Rockpool Bar & Grill
66 Hunter St, Sydney, NSW 2000
1936 Emil Sodersteen

This upmarket bar/restaurant is situated in the City Mutual Building an iconic skyscraper in Sydney.

The gargantuan interior of the restaurant is opulent glamorous and must be on the 'A' list of places to dine when staying in Sydney. The food is divine, and this certainly is a place that you can dress up to the nines.

Regent Cinema
5 Brisbane St, Murwillumbah, NSW 2484
1947 George Rae

Still retaining many of its original features this cinema is the hub of the community. It has regular events and screenings along with a fully licensed bar, where a glass of wine can be enjoyed on the balcony or in the foyer.

Golden Age Cinema
80 Commonwealth St, Surry Hills, Sydney, NSW 2010
1940

This building was originally Paramount House and was utilised as the home of Paramount Pictures' HQ and Newsreel Room up until 1970. It subsequently fell into disrepair and after a full restoration programme reopened in 2013. This independent cinema offers a wide range of films and the bar and screen are located underground.

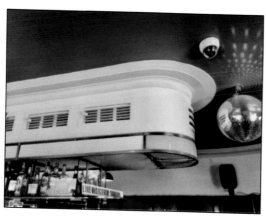

Roxy Community Theatre
114 Pine Ave, Leeton, NSW 2705.
1929-30 Kaberry and Chard

This building was saved and restored by the local community in the 1970s and has been a community theatre ever since. It has subsequently been Heritage Listed and has the capacity for 880 guests. It is an iconic building in Leeton with its large red signage and ornate façade. It offers a year-round programme of theatre, films, and community events.

Enmore Theatre
118-132 Enmore Rd, Newtown, NSW
1930s Charles Bohringer

The Enmore is a renowned music and comedy venue holding up to 2,500 guests. It dates to 1908, and during the 1930s it was extensively renovated with its Art Deco façade. Over the decades it has changed ownership on many occasions, however, it has continually served as an entertainment's venue and is a HeritageLlisted building.

United Cinema
1097 Pittwater Rd, Colloroy, NSW 2097
1938 J.C. Rennie Bartel

This building is a fine example of Streamline Moderne design and originally opened as the De-Lux theatre. It has changed ownership several times over the decades and acquired its vibrant colour that would not be amiss in Miami, and it is conveniently just across from the beach. It is an independent run cinema and offers a full range blockbusters and classic films including some live events. The interior has retained some of its original decorative features and the seating is located on two levels in comfortable larger than average cinema chairs.

Hayden Orpheum
380 Military Rd, Cremorne, NSW 2090
1935 George Newtown Kenworthy

This Heritage Listed independent cinema is a visual feast both externally and interiorly. It not only offers an eclectic mix of movies in its six-screen cinema, it has a piano bar and a live Wurlitzer organ along with special themed nights. One

visit here is not enough to delight in the abundant Art Deco features.

Hayden Orpheum interior lighting

Minerva Metro Cinema/Theatre
Orwell Street, Potts Point, NSW 2011
1939 C. Bruce Dellit

From 1939 to 1950 this iconic venue was a well-established playhouse that dazzled everyone who visited including the big stars of the day. It was in 1950 that Metro-Goldwyn-Mayer took over the Minerva and renamed it the Metro continuing its heyday. During the 1970s it was starting to flag and it reverted to a live Theatre venue attracting the likes of Ginger Rogers when she visited Sydney, she performed here elevating the Minerva and temporary bringing it back into the limelight.

THEATRE ACTION GROUP
RECLAIMING THE METRO, KINGS CROSS

©Frank Van Straten

The last show at the Metro Minerva was in 1977. In the early 1980s George Miller acquired the building and used it as a film studio for films such as Babe and the Mel Gibson Mad Max series. George Miller sold the Metro building in 2018 to property developers, rightfully this caused grave concerns for the future of this national treasure and the Community Minerva Theatre Action Group were formed, consisting of a team of specialist historians and individuals. The aim is to fully restore the Minerva back to its origins and reopen it as a multi-functional venue without losing its integrity and history.

Powerhouse Museum
500 Harris St, Ultimo, NSW 2007

MAAS (Museum of Applied Arts & Sciences) is compiled of the Powerhouse Museum, Sydney Observatory and Museums Discovery Centre. All three are worth visiting, however, the highlight is the Kings Cinema permanent exhibition at the Powerhouse Museum. It consists of an amalgamation of sadly demolished Art

Deco cinemas and pieces them together with authentic newsreel and films from the period. It is a work of art seeing the foyer of the former Kings cinema (*1939 Guy Crick & Bruce Furse*) that includes interior fittings from the Queen Victoria Building. The seats inside are from the Manly Odeon, built in 1932 and demolished in 1985.

You can experience the enchanting sounds of the mechanical music maker called a Foto plate that accompanied the silent films. It is a stark reminder of the Heritage that has been lost, however, it highlights and champions the campaigns and importance of saving our existing Art Deco Heritage for future generations. Open seven days a week 10am-5pm.

Ritz Cinema
45 St Pauls St, Randwick, NSW 2031
1937 Aaron Bolot

This independent Heritage Listed cinema screens mainstream and art house films. It offers the full package experience as both inside and out have the original features. It has a bar and dining that can be enjoyed on the balcony.

Crest Cinema
157 Blaxcell St, Granville, City of Parramatta, NSW
1948 Cowper, Murphy & Associates

It is the imposing, striking fin tower and corner entrance of this building that encapsulates the design style of the Interwar era. Albeit this being a 1948 construction is testimony to its popularity and longevity as a supreme design style. It operated as a cinema until 1963 owned by the Hoyts Theatres chain until its purpose changed to a ballroom and bingo hall. Today the building is used as a public hall.

Former Savoy Theatre
54 Dalgarno St, Coonabarabran, NSW 2357
1941 Crick & Furse

This building operated as an independent cinema until 1970s when it closed. It has been utilised as a roller skating and dance centre and is now a new and used clothing store. It is a Heritage Listed site, and it is of particular interest as little has been changed exteriorly or interiorly since its inauguration.

Orion Function Centre
155 Beamish St, Sydney, NSW 2194
1936

This former theatre is now utilised as a glamorous function centre catering for up to 550 guests. It is popular for weddings, private parties and hosting business events. The stage is also available to hire by independent theatre companies for concerts and performances.

State Theatre Building
49 Market St, Sydney, NSW 2000
1929 Henry Eli White

The extravagant interior of the State Theatre is a fusion of architectural and design styles incorporating Gothic, Baroque, French Empire and Art Deco. The building is privately owned and since 1974 it has hosted the Sydney Film Festival. It can boast having one of only three 21 Rank Wurlitzers and a Koh-i-Noor cut crystal chandelier weighing over four tonnes. Above the Theatre are a further 11 storeys and these now house offices although originally it was a shopping arcade with over 150 shops served by lifts. It has been a Heritage Listed building since 1999.

ANZAC War Memorial and Pool of Reflection
Liverpool St, Hyde Park, Sydney, NSW 2000
1934 C. Dellit & G. Rayner Hoff

In 1916 fundraising began for a memorial to acknowledge the first anniversary of the Australian and New Zealand Army Corps landing at Anzac Cove for the battle of Gallipoli.

The memorial and message that it conveys is exceedingly powerful through the design; Charles Bruce Dellit was the architect and George Rayner Hoff was responsible for the monumental sculptures and reliefs.

It is mammoth in size and constructed of concrete with a pink granite exterior cladding and Art Deco features of setbacks, buttresses and a ziggurat inspired stepped roof.

The white marble faced interior with a domed ceiling is adorned with 120,000 gold stars representing the men and women from New South Wales who served during the first World War. The Anzac Memorial is Heritage Listed and designated a World Heritage site in 2010.

Transport House
19-31 York St, Sydney, NSW 2000
1938 H.E. Budden and Mackey

Transport House was formerly the Railway HQ and it is a fine example of commercial architecture during the 1930s and was well received, despite its initial critics who felt disdain due to the use of day labour during its construction. It won awards for its design including a RIBA medal in 1939. The 12-story framed structure has horizontal bands of large bronze framed windows. The lower façade is clad in green terracotta tiles.

Mutual Life and Citizens Building
42-46 Martin Place, Sydney, NSW 2000
1938 Emil Sodersten

Boldly inscribed with the MLC abbreviation this skyscraper building rose 46 metres the highest allowed at the time, with a further 15 metres gained from the tower. It was the Mutual Life and Citizens Assurance Company head office and its grandeur announced to the world how prosperous and important the company were. Consisting of 11 floors the upper are clad in buff sandstone and polished rose red granite is used for the plinth course beneath the windows and around the doorways on the ground level. The entrance sculpture is by Rayner Hoft who was responsible for the sculptures around the ANZAC War Memorial in Hyde Park, Sydney. The building is currently occupied by a Law firm.

Sydney Dental Hospital
2 Chalmers St, Surry Hills, NSW 2010
1940 Stephenson & Turner

This exceptional building is a fine example of Streamline Moderne design. The architects were a local Sydney firm and it still retains its resplendent ability to enthral the public, especially as it is located opposite the entrance to the Central Railway Station, such a fine site to be greeted by. It is still a thriving Dental Hospital and is affiliated to the dentistry teaching department University of Sydney.

University House
300 King St, Newcastle, NSW 2300
1939 Emil Sodersteen

This building was originally constructed for the Newcastle Electricity Supply Council Administration. The interior included offices and accommodation for staff, a showroom and demonstration theatre.

Over the years it has been remodelled with the tower being added in 1967. Its history includes being home to a radio station, and an architectural practice prior to being established as a library for the University of Newcastle in 1995. The main buildings framework is concrete encased steel with concrete flooring. Since 1999 it has been Heritage Listed.

Macleay -Regis Apartment Building
12 Macleay St, Potts Point, Sydney, NSW 2011
1939 Pitt & Phillips

This large apartment building is known to be compared with the Rockefeller Apartments on 54th Street, New York, that were constructed in 1936. The architectural plans for the Rockefeller were reviewed in journals that would have been freely available to Pitt & Phillips and this could have heavily influenced the design with the architects, however, this has never been proven.

The building today is practically the same as when it opened in 1939, the striking quadrant-shaped balconies making it stand out from its neighbours and the Art Deco inspired detailing on the exterior of the building includes the parapets above the projecting bays and the central portico. The interior of the apartments has been adapted and altered over the ensuing years. The opulent foyer is fitting of such a statement building.

Luna Park
1 Olympic Dr, Milson Point, Sydney, NSW 2061
1935 Rupert Browne & Herman Phillips

Opening in 1935 this small 330-metre-long amusement park was based on the first Luna Park that opened on Coney Island, New York, back in 1903. It is owned and run by the Luna Park Reserve Trust and has the only surviving operational wooden wild mouse rollercoaster ride in the world (Luna Sydney acquired it in 1962).

The Ferris wheel offers great views of the harbour and the Coney Island section of the park located in the centre is a separate pay feeing area (included in a day pass) and offers a full on vintage experience of original vintage attractions. It is pleasingly ungated, and you can pay by ride, buy a day pass or just meander through and enjoy the atmosphere. This theme park is a wonderful nostalgic trip and the murals and paintwork on the sets and equipment are fantastic. Highly recommend visiting both day and night-time to experience the illuminations and small parades.

Sydney Harbour Bridge
Bradfield Hwy, Dawes Point – Milsons Point, Sydney, NSW 2061
1932 constructed by Dorman Long & Co

Sydney Harbour Bridge is the main artery for traffic and to and from the city and it now consists of eight vehicle lanes, two train lines, a footway, and a cycleway. Made of steel with concrete abutments it took six years to construct and has a colossal 6 million hand driven rivets. The general design was drawn up by Dr J. Bradfield and officers at the board of the NSW Department of Public Works and the finer details were undertaken by the contractors consulting engineer Ralph Freeman and his associate Mr G. Imbault. After inviting worldwide tenders in 1922 the overall build of the bridge was given to the British firm Dorman Long of Middlesbrough who incorporated elements of the 1928 Tyne Bridge in

Newcastle-upon-Tyne. The southern end of the bridge is located at Dawes Point in The Rocks area, and the northern end at Milsons Point in the lower North Shore area. The four decorative 89-metre-high pylons are made of concrete, faced with granite quarried from nearby Morouya. A walking trip is available to visit the South Eastern Pylon which involves a long walk to the base of the pylon then a further 200 steps to the top. You do need to be reasonably fit, however, the rewards you will reap will be worth every bit of the effort.

Bondi Icebergs Pool
1 Notts Avenue, Bondi Beach, NSW 2026

The famous Bondi Baths as they are known have been in existence for over 100 years and is an historic landmark. In 1929 the Iceberg Club was formed for enthusiastic swimmers wishing to stay fit during the winter months, since the 1940's a strict code applies to becoming an officiated member called the 15B rule. Members have to swim at least 3 Sundays out of 4, for 5 years before officially deemed as an Iceberg member and joining the ranks.

©Archives Iceberg Club

The large lap pool and children's pool are open to the public with breath-taking views and the overall experience of swimming in this pool next to the ocean with waves lapping by your side is unforgettable. Originally the buildings were large tin huts, it was during the 1960's and 1970's that the purpose-built construction took place and this sits proudly alongside the large pools. Changing rooms, sauna and showers are included in the admission fee and a café/restaurant overlooks the pool on the upper floor of the building.

Sydney Opera House
Bennelong Point, Sydney, NSW 2000

Complementing the Sydney Harbour Bridge and Luna Park situated on the opposite bank on Bennelong Point is the Expressionist ground-breaking, Sydney Opera House. This monumental building was designed by Jørn Utzon and the structural engineer Ove Arup who was a master in his field and instrumental in engineering this complex structure. Construction started in 1959 and was completed in 1973 it is owned by NSW Government.

Located a fifteen-minute ferry ride around Sydney harbour is the pleasant district of Double Bay. The area can boast of some impressive housing and it has earned its name by the locals of 'double bay, double pay' as real estate is above the average price. You will be rewarded for your short trip as you get a fabulous view of the Sydney Opera House and Bridge from the water. The pace in Double Bay is much slower than central Sydney and you can take a leisurely few hour on the upward incline to discover Art Deco buildings both residential and retail, you'll even discover an Art Deco small electrical sub-station.

Australian Capital Territory (ACT)

Capital City - Canberra
Territorial Bird - Gang-gang Cockatoo
Territorial Flower - Royal Bluebell
Area Total - 910 square miles

ACCOMMODATION

The Kurrajong
8 National Circuit, Barton, Canberra, ACT 2600
1926 John Smith Murdoch

J.S. Murdoch was the Commonwealth Chief Architect who is also famous for designing Old Parliament House. The property is steeped in political history and was a residence for Members of Parliament and Public Servants. Prime Minister Ben Chifley lived here throughout his career which included his term in office from 1945-49 and up until his death in 1951. As described by the establishment its roots are reflected in the Art Deco decor, nostalgic ambient lighting, jazz music and lounge filled with books and artworks.

Hyatt Hotel Canberra
120 Commonwealth Ave, Canberra ACT 2600
1924 John Smith Murdoch

This Heritage hotel has retained its 1920s elegance whilst incorporating modern Art Deco designs. The 252 guest rooms and suites are exceptionally stylish and luxurious, and a favourite is the king bed with balcony as the Italian marble bathroom and beautiful views are unsurpassed. An afternoon tea in the Tea Lounge is *de rigueur* and the Speaker's Corner Bar conjures up conversations of old. A gentle morning and evening dip in the inviting swimming indoor pool makes this a memorable stay.

Deco Hotel
214 Northbourne Ave, Braddon, ACT 2612

The Deco Hotel was purpose built and opened in 2019 and certainly earns its place here not purely on its name but on its definition of its Functionalist style. It would not look out of place in Dessau, Germany with its pleasing stripped back design and equally as inviting interior. It has 210 guest rooms and suites spread over seven floors all adhering to minimalist clean lines and modernist interior design a hit with the Bauhausian set.

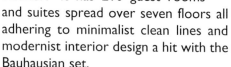

West Block of Old Parliament House
King George Terrace, Parkes, Canberra, ACT 2600

In 2017 the multimillion-dollar project to turn the vacant west block of Old Parliament House into a luxury hotel began. This historic building was designed by the architect John Smith Murdoch and opened in 1927 as part of the Secretariat building and amongst other uses it was home to the National Library. The historic values of this site are to be celebrated by the property developers Geocon who want the public to enjoy the authentic structure inside and out which is a version of the Interwar Stripped Classical style. Watch this space for developments!

OUT AND ABOUT

National Film and Sound Archive
McCoy Circuit, Acton, Canberra, ACT 2601

This building started life as the Australian Institute of Anatomy and is Interwar Stripped Classical in style rather than Art Deco opening in 1931. However, it does incorporate many Art Deco features and elements with the classical columns, horizontal lines, flat roof, and stone carved motifs/bas-reliefs.

It was in 1984 that the National Film and Sound Archive was established in the building with over 2 million listed works in the form of films and sound. During 2019 the sandstone façade was renovated giving it a new gleaming brilliance, and you will be delighted to find that in the foyer decorative Aboriginal art and motifs are present along with native flora and fauna displayed on the building's exterior. This venue is most definitely worth a visit.

Australian War Memorial
Treloar Cres, Campbell, ACT 2612
Construction started 1928 Emil Sodersten & John Crust

This colossal shrine and extensive museum built in the Art Deco and Byzantine architectural styles pays homage to the country's military services and sacrifices. Its mission in leading remembrance and understanding of Australia's wartime experience is certainly captured and conveyed in this goliath structure.

Museum of Australian Democracy - Old Parliament House
18 King George Terrace, Parkes, ACT 2600
1927 John Smith Murdoch

The Old Parliament House building was the original seat of the Federal Parliament until 1988 when it relocated to its new premises on Capital Hill. The building now houses the Museum of Australian Democracy and is an engaging and stimulating place to visit for its architecture and story that unfolds within. With its changing and permanent exhibitions, along with tours that include the Indigenous experiences of democracy, and a Top-Secret tour, make this a fun and educational day out. This experience can all be topped off with a nice lunch in the restaurant.

John Gorton Building
Parkes Pl, Parkes, ACT, 2600
1956 George Sydney Jones

From its inception in 1924 until its completion in 1956 this Interwar Stripped Classical Style administration building displays some fine features. The lengthy build was partly due to financial constraints and secondly by shoddy workmanship that compromised the foundation and work had to be halted. Originally it was occupied by the News and Information Bureau then subsequently by Government departments and was renamed in 1999 to the John Gorton building after the 19th Prime Minister.

Robert Marsden Hope Building
2 National Circuit, Barton, ACT 2600

This Government owned building was completed in 1940 and currently houses the Office of National Assessments. From its inception until 1971 it housed the Patent Office; it is a Heritage Listed property and was fully renovated in 2013. The impressive structure consists of three floors and is constructed of concrete, sandstone cladding, marble and steel.

© *National Library of Australia*

VICTORIA STATE

Capital - Melbourne
State Bird - Helmeted Honeyeater
State Flower - Common Heath
Total Area - 87,806 square miles

ACCOMMODATION

Park Hyatt Hotel
1 Parliament Place, East, Melbourne, VIC 3002

This luxury hotel is a mixture of Victorian and Modern architecture with the interior strongly veering towards Art Deco in fixtures and fittings. It has 240 elegant guest rooms and lavish suites. It is a five-star high end property with two restaurants, a pool and spa, and possesses that overall wow factor for luxury and decadence that one would expect from the jazz age.

The Prince Hotel
2 Acland St, St Kilda, VIC 3182

A hotel has stood on this site since the mid-1800s and in 1936 it was rebuilt in the fashionable Art Deco style by the prolific architect Robert H McIntyre. Located along the beach in St Kilda often referred to a Melbourne's *playground by the sea*, the hotel has a perfect location. The guest rooms are all

tastefully decorated and furnished in a soft palette. The hospitality and service is second to none in this outstanding building.

Shamrock Hotel
120 Mollison St, Kyneton, VIC 3444
1867

The Shamrock is a welcoming historic spot that was originally established in 1867 and updated during the interwar period with its Streamline exterior.

It has on offer great food and refreshing beers and is welcoming to both locals and visitors. It does offer some accommodation, and this is available via direct request to the hotel.

Golden Age Hotel/Motel
Tongio Rd, Omeo, VIC 3898
1939

This great property that was built in 1939 after a bush fire destroyed the previous building, offers accommodation to suit all budgets, with its two luxury spa units, 13 motel units and six pub style rooms.

The restaurant offers a full a la carte menu and is fully stocked with wines and beers. The surroundings and staff are exceptionally welcoming and friendly, making this a fabulous place to spend time at while exploring the area.

The Fish Creek Hotel
1 Old Waratah Rd, Fish Creek, VIC 3959
1939

The Fish Creek Hotel opened in 1939, and has nine retro motel units available that are located behind the hotel and an additional seven guest rooms upstairs in the main building.

These are comfortably furnished with recent renovations completed. Spacious areas include a relaxed lounge, bar, and restaurant with excellent local sourced food.

Ararat Hotel
130 Barkly St, Ararat, VIC 3377

With its impressive exterior of speed lines and curvilinear features the Ararat is certainly a treasure to look at. It offers a full menu and bar along with budget guest rooms with shared facilities.

OUT AND ABOUT

Terminus Hotel
605 Victoria Street, Abbotsford VIC 3067

The Terminus certainly sets the standards high as this restaurant/pub is an absolute dream both outside and in. Its unmissable as you approach, as it certainly makes a delightful statement on Victoria Street and this continues inside the building as the tiled walls and fittings are all in keeping with the period.

Loddon Bridge Hotel
2 Main St, Bridgwater on Loddon, VIC 3516
1940

This Pub was built in 1940 and is a showcase of Interwar design with the exterior featuring a wide central spandrel rising from the main doorway. It does not have guest rooms, however, nearby just across the bridge accommodation is available. It does great food and beer and the setting is great along the Loddon River.

The Orrong Hotel
709 High St, Armadale, Melbourne, VIC 3143

This impressive building alas is not a hotel; however, it does serve a good dinner and beer. The exterior is an absolute joy incorporating curvilinear features, fin towers, speed lines and ziggurats.

Former Clifton Motors
205-211 Queens Parade, Clifton Hill, VIC 3068
1939 James Wardrop

Immediately recognisable with its central fin display this building which is formerly Clifton Motors and until mid-2020 was operating as a restaurant; is currently up for lease or purchase while going to press.

The interior has been adapted for purpose over the years and little remains of its original features. However, the exterior is impressive, and it would be a delight to see the interior refitted in Art Deco style.

McDonalds Clifton Hill
199 Queens Parade, Fitzroy North VIC 3068
1937 James Wardrop

This iconic building originally the United Kingdom hotel must questioningly be one of the most beautiful settings to indulge in fast food.

It is a real showstopper of a building with its central fin and patterned brickwork. Even if you are not a fan of the big whopper, you cannot miss the opportunity of stepping inside to gloat and partaking in a vege deluxe!

Sebastian Restaurant
26 Esplanade, Williamstown, VIC 3016
1936 Bridge & Bogle

The beach pavilion on the esplanade is home to the welcoming and stylish Sebastian bar and restaurant.

This satisfying building can accommodate many guests inside and has the bonus of outside veranda seating.

Sipping cocktails and watching the sunset in such beautiful surroundings does not get much better than this.

Ilona Staller Restaurant
282 Carlisle St, Balaclava, VIC 3183

This Italian restaurant located in the former Commonwealth Bank complete with curved bar is delightful.

The interior was tastefully and sympathetically remodelled in 2012 to accommodate repurposing the building.

Palais Theatre
Lower Esplanade, St Kilda, Melbourne, VIC 3182
1927 Henry E. White

When visiting Melbourne, the Palais Theatre must be on the top of your list of places to visit. It is considered to be the number *'must see'* theatre with its rich history of hosting both homegrown and international names.

The current Palais sits on the site of two previous theatres (one which burnt down just prior to completion) and is currently being fully renovated. Phase one restoring the exterior of the building has now been completed and phase two is waiting to begin. This will involve restoring the large domed ceiling, and updating the internal facilities. This is a true showstopper of a theatre and has the capacity to seat 2,896 people. Be prepared to be entertained by the building, let alone the performance.

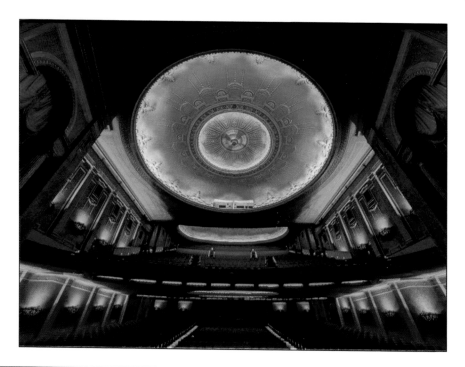

Sun Theatre

8 Ballarat St, Yarraville, VIC 3013

1938 Cowper, Murphy & Appleford

After its rise and fall over the decades and ongoing wrangles to save it from demolition and redevelopment the Sun Theatre is once again flourishing.

With a capacity to seat 1050 guests and with all of the original Art Deco architecture that has not been compromised by adding new auditoriums this is a success story. With a diverse programme appealing to all ages and audiences the dedicated team who oversee and run the Theatre they have succeeded in making it a great entertainment venue.

Village Cinemas Rivoli
200 Camberwell Rd, Hawthorn East, Melbourne, VIC 3123
1940 H. Vivian Taylor & Soilleaux

This cinema certainly celebrates the Art Deco style in exuberance with its large 8

screen multiplex located in suburb of Melbourne. It reopened its doors in 2000 following a full renovation and expansion project. The original screen in the circle area still retains its 1940s decorative detail and comfortably seats nearly 500 guests.

If you want to experience a wonderful nostalgic evening out, then definitely head for the Rivoli and spend time before your movie to soak up the atmosphere and have a coffee or glass of wine admiring the glorious surroundings from the roof garden and bar.

Astor Theatre
1 Chapel Street, St Kilda, Victoria 3182
1935 Ron Morton Taylor

This is the last single screen cinema of its kind in continuous operation in Melbourne, still standing since its grand opening in 1936, and one of only a few single screen movie theatres from the 1930s in the world screening repertory movie programming. It is fully air conditioned and is famous for its mix of classic, cult and new release movies. There is nothing "old-fashioned" about the Astor's facilities, however, as it is fully-air-conditioned and can boast a state-of-the-art sound system and a giant screen.

Her Majesty's Theatre
219 Exhibition Street, Melbourne, VIC 3000
1934 C.N. Hollinshed & Walkley

HMT as it is known dates to 1886 with its elegant façade and it was in 1934 that the interior was totally redesigned and renovated by the prolific architects and designers Hollinshed & Walkley to the high standard of lavish Art Deco that we see today.

In 2000 it was purchased by Mike Walsh a former Australian radio and television presenter and it was refitted to accommodate larger productions. Be prepared to be dazzled by the intensity of opulence and glamour in the large auditorium that seats 1,700 guests.

Palace Westgarth Cinema
89 High Street, Northcote, VIC 3070
1921 John Secull

The Palace Westgarth is situated in the Northcote district of Melbourne and combines 1920's classical features with Art Deco and Modernistic styling.

With five opulent auditoria and two stylish bars this cinema qualifies as an 'A' lister to visit.

Luna Park
18 Lower Esplanade, St Kilda, VIC 3182

This recreational theme park was the first Luna to open in Australia on December 13th, 1912. The now famous Mr Moon mouth had over twenty-two thousand people walk through who each paid sixpence to enter. Visitors could enjoy the grand carousal, rollercoaster rides and see high wire trapeze artists, and original footage from the opening day is available to view on the Luna Park website.

Chemistry Building
The University of Melbourne, Masson Road, Parkville, VIC 3052
1938 Percy Everett, Public Works Department

Of significant historic importance and listed on the National Trust Register this cream brickwork Chemistry building is described as a Modernist Interwar building incorporating Gothic architecture. Its impact is in the massing that is balanced by the detailed tower features. The interior of the building has been adapted for modern day technology.

Second Church of Christ Scientist
Cookson Street, Camberwell
1934-36 Bates, Smart & McCutcheon

This statement structure cost £13,998 to build during 1934-36 by the Hansen and Yuncken P/L company. The final figure amounted to £19,660 after the internal fixtures including the organ were installed and the Architects received the Royal Victorian Institute of Architects Award in 1938 for the building's simplicity, architectural dignity and use of massing amongst other identified qualities.

©Heritage Council Victoria

Shopping Arcade
Manchester Unity, 220-226 Collins St,
Melbourne, VIC 3002
1932 Marcus Barlow

In the suburbs of Melbourne, you will find exclusive large Art Deco Streamline Moderne residential properties that fetch a tidy sum. A prime example of one of these is the Mon Reve House on Hampden Road, Armadale, Melbourne it was built in 1937 by the architect I.G. Anderson and it is well worth a drive out to view.

If you want to experience some homegrown football then look no further than the Hawkes Hawthorn Footy Club at 34 Linda Crescent, Hawthorn and you will be pleasantly surprised with the Glenferrie Oval Grandstand designed in 1938 by Stuart Calder with its sweeping canopy. As you will find Melbourne is a hot bed of Art Deco and when visiting any new region it is always worth seeking out the Art Deco Society, Twentieth Century Society or local guides and walking tours within that place as they are a mind of useful information and have the expertise and knowledge of the vast amount on offer on their patch.

Epworth Freemasons Hospital
Clarendon Street, East Melbourne, VIC 3002
1936-37 Stephenson & Meldrum

This Functionalist Modern style building incorporates bold horizontal balconies with a contrasting vertical service tower and minimal decoration.

It was extended sympathetically during 1956-58 and further additions were added in 1968. The white rendered exterior was trimmed with blue tiles and horizontal tubular steel balustrades, the original main entrance was altered in 1977, however, this building is a valued prime example of interwar architecture adapted to cater for modern day use.

St Vincent's Private Hospital (Mercy Hospital)
159 Grey St, East Melbourne, VIC 3002
1934-36 Stephenson & Meldrum

This hospital along with many others around the globe was established by the Sisters of Mercy whose founder member Catherine McAuley was born in Dublin,

Ireland in 1778 and dedicated her life to caring for the sick and poor, especially women. This Functionalist and Modernist Interwar building incorporates different architectural elements and is now a Private Hospital that specialises in women's health.

Brunswick Fire Station and flats
24 Blyth Street, Brunswick, VIC 3056
1937-38 Seabrook & Fildes

This fire station was the first in Melbourne to embrace the Functionalist Interwar style and included accommodation at the back of the station for the fireman and their families. The structure has horizontal window banding with cantilevered hooded fenestrations and impressive brickwork.

Royal Historical Society of Victoria Headquarters
249 A'Beckett Street, Melbourne, VIC 3000
1938 George Hallandal

This exemplary building comprises of brick and plaster and the strong vertical and horizontal lines with elongated windows certainly make it stand out from the crowd. The overall building is Functionalist and Utilitarian in design and was built for the Australian Army Medical Corps, as a Drill Hall and operated in this capacity until 1988. During 1999 the Royal Historical Society of Victoria took up residence in the western end of the premises and several times a year an exhibition is held in the building.

© *Royal Historical Society*

General Motors Holden
Salmon Street, Fishermen's Bend, Melbourne, VIC, 3001
1937 Eric Gibson & John Storey

General Motors Holden originally started out as a saddlery business in the nineteenth century diversifying into vehicle upholstery and the full-scale production of cars (including tramcars during the 1920s for Melbourne).

© *National Trust Australia*

The factory at Salmon Street was an assembly plant and new Headquarters therefore reflecting the status, importance and success of the business akin to a State Government Building. The colossal scale of the entire site includes large parking areas and eventually totalled over 39 hectares. The uniformity, set-backs, horizontals, verticals and central tower with motifs elevate this building to national importance and it is a listed National Trust Heritage site. It was during 2013 that the Holden Company advised they would cease trading by 2017 and the Government of Victoria paid $130 million dollars in 2016 for the entire site with a thirty-year redevelopment plan of residential housing and infrastructure.

The Capitol Building
109-117 Swanson Street
1924 W. Burley Griffin and Marion Mahoney Griffin

The Capitol building is flanked by the so called 'Barlow Bookends' of the Manchester Unity and the Century Building resembling radiators. This 11-storey building was purchased by the RMIT University in 1999 to use as a lecture venue for the students. The University partnered with Six Degrees Architects to reconstruct the theatre space as the building is comprised of residential apartments, office space and a large basement and arcade. Due to regulations and financial constraints the further renovation programme to the theatre was stalled until the latter part of the 2010's.

The capacity for the theatre is 600, originally it had over 2000 seats, however, following the controversial significant reconstruction in 1968 some of the finer features were lost and readapted. The theatre is now a learning venue by day and a building for Melbournians during the evening offering mixed media and cultural events to the public.

The *piece de la resistance* is the ceiling of the theatre that was described by the architects as the 'Crystaline Cave' and this is mainly attributed to Marion Mahoney Griffin. She met her husband Walter Burley Griffin when they were students of Frank Lloyd Wright and she worked in Lloyd Wright's offices for over 10 years.

Mitchell House
352-362, Lonsdale Street, Melbourne, VIC 3000
1936 Harry Norris

This Heritage Listed Streamline Moderne building was originally designed to be ten storeys, however, only six storeys were built.

It is utilised as commercial office space and the desirable features incorporated include the curvilinear corners and windows with an asymmetrical tower and spandrels.

St Anne's Apartment Block
1 Park St, South Yarra, VIC 3141
1935 J. Edmond Dorney

Located on the corner of Park Street and Toorak Road West, the substantial and impressive apartment block of St Anne's can be found. These properties are highly desirable in a leafy suburb of Melbourne, and all around this area an eclectic mix of high-end properties of different architectural styles are positioned.

Commonwealth Bank of Australia
219-225 Bourke St, Melbourne, VIC 3000
1939-41 H.M. Rolland

The former Commonwealth Bank of Australia is an 11-storey high office building and is described by the Victorian Heritage Database as being in the Interwar Stripped Classical style and an example of the Commercial Palazzo type, which also reflects the progressive styles of the 1930s: the abstraction of classical elements of the Stripped Classical style, and the dominant vertical expression of the Streamlined Moderne style. It has only recently been Heritage Listed after a long campaign from the Art Deco and Modernism Society of Australia who highlighted its plight along with many other significant buildings over the years ensuring the rich architectural Heritage of Melbourne is retained for Australia and the World to enjoy.

Manchester Unity Tower
220-226 Collins St, Melbourne VIC 300
1932 Marcus Barlow

This is the most iconic building in Melbourne due to its Heritage, which encompasses art, culture, commerce, and science. It was built as the new headquarters of the Manchester Unity Independent Order of Odd Fellows (IOOF) who were a non-profit friendly society whose doctrine followed a strong sense of tradition and the noble motto of the society was 'Friendship, Love and Truth'.

Spanning 12 floors this Gothic stepped architectural feast is constructed of concrete-encased steel and the exterior is clad in 250 tons of terracotta faience tiles. Throughout the building be prepared for Australian marbles on interior walls, lavish lighting and the 11th floor boardroom complete with its Art Deco fireplace and wood veneered panelling.

The *1932* Café & Restaurant are located in the arcade of the building and has an Art Deco inspired interior, one hour guided tours of the building are also available and can be combined with lunch.

Kodak House
252 Collins Street, Melbourne, VIC 3000
1934-5 Oakley & Parkes

This building was the first to use stainless steel on the spandrels depicting the Kodak signage and the large quantities of steel, polished red granite and terracotta exterior all contribute to making this an exceptional and fascinating building. It was utilised as a retail outlet, sales offices, and camera repairs were carried out on the 3rd floor.

A rich interior of glass fixtures, brass, and wood were all prevalent back in its heyday, however, following major interior renovations in the 1950s the majority of these were lost. The company was flourishing and in 1979 the Kodak offices relocated to bigger premises and it was in 1983 when eventually the retail shop closed at the site.

Alkira House – Bond Street Kitchen Cafe
18 Queen Street, Melbourne, VIC 3000
1936-37 James Wardrop

This outstanding Heritage Listed building is the former Electricity Commission Offices. One of its claims to fame is that it was the first building in Australia to use glass bricks in its construction. With its use of glazed

terracotta tiles in black and white vertical strips it leads the eye to its summit. It is now comprised of private apartments and a café on the ground floor.

Australian Catholic Assurance Co. Ltd.,
118-126 Queen Street, Melbourne
1936-7 Hennessy, Hennessy & Co. with R Morton Taylor

The ACA building is striking with its vertical ribs resembling what is known as 'Commercial Gothic'. It incorporates setbacks on the upper levels and the eye is always drawn upwards to the central tower. Interestingly instead of using a cement render an artificial stone product 'Benedict Stone' was utilised. Integrated with a darker shade of stone at the lower levels and subtly lighter stone travelling to the top brightens and heightens the building. This stone was manufactured by a company owned by the Brisbane Diocese of the Catholic Church.

The Centre Ivanhoe
275 Upper Heidelberg Rd, Ivanhoe, VIC 3079
1937 Leith & Bartlett with Peck & Kettering

This function centre is a fine example of Art Deco architecture with its five venue rooms (that can accommodate from 80 to 800 guests), stages and large parquetry dance floors that can be hired for community or individual events. In certain

areas of the venue it is currently undergoing a $29 million upgrade to deliver the new Ivanhoe Library and Cultural Hub.

Civic Hall Ballarat
300/304 Mair St, Ballarat Central, VIC 3350
1953 Herbert 'Les' Coburn & Gordon Murphy

This Government owned building has recently in 2019 undergone a full restoration programme. It hosts a diverse entertainment programme throughout the year and has a total venue capacity of 2,000 people.

© Ballarat, Victoria Government

TASMANIA

Capital City - Hobart
State Animal - Tasmanian Devil
State Flower - Tasmanian Blue Gum
Area Total - 68,401 square miles

© Australian National Botanic Gardens Gov. AU

ACCOMMODATION

Alabama Hotel
72 Liverpool St, Hobart, TAS 7000.

The building at the Alabama dates to the 1830's and it was in 1867 that it was transformed into a hotel. During the 1930's it was modernised with the impressive Art Deco façade being added. It has 17 comfortable guest rooms with shared facilities; however, the male and female showers are separate. It has some touches of deco and vintage within the bedrooms and public areas. It is friendly welcoming hotel and convenient if you are on a tight budget.

Neptune Grand Hotel (aka The Happy Backpackers Penguin)
84 Main Rd, Penguin, TAS, 7316
1938

Located next to the beachside this is a great budget price hotel ideal for a stopover or extended few days. It offers simplicity and high standards with shared bathroom facilities and good Asian Australian inspired food in the restaurant.

OUT & ABOUT

Telegraph Hotel
19 Morrison St, Hobart, TAS 7000

The Telegraph pub is no exception to the rule, as like many of the pubs in Australia constructed during the interwar years, it is built on the convergence of two roads. Making a statement with its sweeping Streamline contours. This popular pub offers a good array of beers and food in convivial surroundings.

The Winston
381 Elizabeth St, North Hobart, TAS 7000

The Winston pub/restaurant is a good old-fashioned eatery serving great food and beer in a jovial setting. The original windows and decorative façade features of the speed lines make this building shine above the rest.

Star Theatre
217b Invermay Rd, Invermay, Launceston, TAS 7248
1937 Guy Crick

This delightful historic theatre originally seated 852 guests opening in October 1937. It has not lost its appeal, and after restoration it now comfortably seats 250 guests who can enjoy a light meal accompanied by a good selection of wines. The exterior combines elements of Streamline Moderne and Art Deco reflecting the golden age of cinema.

Holyman House
52 Brisbane St, Launceston, TAS 7250
1936 H.S. East & R. Sharrington Smith

Standing five blocks up and is situated in the business district of Launceston this building originally housed the business branches of Holyman's shipping and aviation interests.

In addition, a showroom for the car division was incorporated on the ground floor.

It is constructed with a modern steel frame and is well loved by locals and nationals, as its flamboyant style incorporates a neo-lit spire and impressive Art Deco features.

It has changed ownership several times, still retaining its original use as commercial office space.

NEW ZEALAND

Population – 4,822,233 (est. 2020)
National Symbol - Kiwi
Unofficial National Flowers – Silver Fern, Red Pohutukawa and Yellow Kowhai
Land Mass – 103,483 square miles

New Zealand consists of the North and South Islands joined by the Conduit Strait and many smaller islands accessible by ferry. The North Island has a population of 3.81 million with the most populated city being Auckland with over 1.5 million residents. Wellington is the Capital City of New Zealand; however, Napier is unequivocally the Art Deco Capital being the nucleus of Interwar architecture following the disastrous 1931 earthquake which raised the City to the ground.

It was subsequently rebuilt in the fashionable Interwar Art Deco style as the design suited the regulated two storey high buildings and was economical in building materials. The influential celebrated architect Louis Hay (1881-1948) was part of the Napier Reconstruction Committee and he ensured that local architects had control over the rebuilding project. He was also responsible for some of the most iconic buildings in Napier including the National Tobacco Company Building.

ACCOMMODATION
NORTH ISLAND

Hotel Debrett
2 High Street, Auckland Central, Auckland 1010, NZ

Hotel Debrett has a long and colourful history, it started out in 1841 and was one of Auckland's first hotels called the Commercial. It survived two fires, and two rebuilds, before the current building was erected in 1925. Dominion Breweries acquired the hotel in 1959, and after a major renovation it was renamed Hotel Debrett.

In 2007 John Courtney and Michelle Deery bought the building that was now a defunct backpacker's hostel and home to a flock of pigeons. It took almost two years to transform the near ruin into the highly awarded hotel you see today. The interior has a distinctive Art Deco style and feel along with incorporating mid-century furnishings. The 25 guest rooms and suites incorporate high end design style with

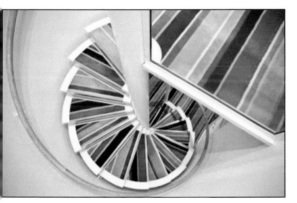

the fixtures and fittings. The décor in the bar is reminiscent of the 1920s and is perfect for evening cocktails. Afternoon tea is served with all the aplomb of a bygone era, and at the heart of the hotel is a modern soaring glass roofed atrium flooding the interior with natural light.

Airedale Boutique Suites
380 Queen St, Auckland, 1010 NZ

Recently undergoing a complete restoration and refurbishment programme the Airedale Boutique Suites (formerly the Scenic Hotel) were constructed in 1946 and offer a distinguished and luxurious stay. Arranged over 10 floors the 97 guest suites are all suitably furnished in contemporary modern style with a nod to Art Deco with the wallpaper and fittings. The Heritage façade can now be fully admired after

decades of dirt have been cleaned away. The Trocadero Restaurant, Bar and the main foyer all possess an element of the hotel's origins.

Grand Hotel Windsor
58/60 Queen St, Auckland, 1001 NZ

Located in a 1928 Heritage Art Deco building this is considered to be Auckland's first skyscraper. The hotel was relaunched in 2017 with the guest rooms and public spaces elegantly and opulently restyled.

The 79 guest rooms and suits offer a luxurious stay and the long-standing Cooke's Restaurant and Bar and are famous for their excellent 'high tea' and surroundings.

Distinction Palmerston North Hotel & Conference Centre
175 Cuba St, Palmerston North, 4441 NZ

This five-storey distinctive building built in 1927 displays a simple yet impressive façade. It offers 85 modern guest rooms with a restaurant and bar. This hotel is a good base to stay at if you are also visiting the Tararua and Ruahine Ranges that have the phenomenal Manawatu Gorge. Nearby attractions also include the New Zealand Rugby Museum.

Meadowood Boutique Accommodation & Venue
1769 Korokipo Rd, Fernhill, Napier, 4138 NZ

The delightful owners of this exceptional 1934 Art Deco home have fully restored the property and were recognised with the prestigious Hastings District Landmarks Art Deco Trust Award in December 2015 for an outstanding project. The property is hired out as a whole and is particularly popular for weddings and family celebrations.

The house itself consists of four very stylish bedrooms with upmarket en-suite facilities. The attention to detail is scrupulous and all the rooms are decorated in the deco style with a theme. Nearby are a good selection of cafes, restaurants, and bars. It is located off State Highway 50, between Hastings and Napier, twelve minutes from Napier airport and a twenty-minute drive to some glorious beaches suitable for swimming.

Deco City Motor Lodge
308 Kennedy Rd, Napier, 4110 NZ

Set in Napier in the Hawke's Bay region this motel offers 30 varied guest rooms. The family apartments are spacious with two bedrooms and lounge, smaller families may

choose the one-bedroom apartments as cots and additional beds are available and the Spa suites are great for couples. The seasonal outdoor pool is most enticing and the add on extras of the free use of bicycles and a playground make this appealing to families and couples.

The Crown Hotel
22A Waghorne St, Ahuriri, Napier, 4144 NZ

Located on the waterfront this Heritage Listed hotel constructed in 1932 has a Spanish Mission façade with a modern extension. It has 39 highly appointed guest rooms and particularly appealing are the Heritage suites with luxury interiors and *Juliette* balconies.

Criterion Hotel
48 Emerson St, Hawkes Bay, Napier, 4144 NZ

A hotel has stood on this site since 1874 and following the 1931 Hawke's Bay earthquake a new Criterion hotel was resurrected in 1933. It has an impressive Spanish Mission façade and sits nicely along Emerson street which is one of the main thoroughfares of shops and eateries. Catering for mainly backpackers this hostel has a separate male and female dormitory and 25 guest rooms with shared facilities (limited amount include en-suite). It has two flights of stairs and no lift/elevator so bear this in mind if you have heavy luggage. The shared lounge and kitchen facilities are good, and the open balcony is a delight.

Masonic Hotel
2 Tennyson St, Napier 4110 NZ
1936 Peter Daleissi

The Masonic Hotel is synonymous with Napier and a hotel has stood on this site since 1876, it was rebuilt in 1936 due to a fire. In 2008 the hotel underwent major renovations, and its 43 guest rooms are highly sought after especially during the Art Deco festivals in February and July. Features include a sweeping staircase and luxurious décor with a popular bar and restaurant. The large Art Deco Suite on the first floor overlooks the promenade with fine views.

The County Hotel
12 Browning St, Napier South, Napier, 4110 NZ

This hotel is only one of two significant buildings that survived the 1931 earthquake and dates to 1909 when it was built for the County Council.

It is in the centre of Napier and has an Edwardian Art Deco glamour with furnishings and fittings. The 18 guest rooms offer luxury and style along with the highly acclaimed restaurant, champagne snug bar, lounge and library.

The Dome
101 Marine Parade, Napier, Hawke's Bay, 4110 NZ

This 1935 building was originally the Temperance General Insurance, a company who emerged from the prohibition era that took place in the earlier part of the 1900s. The corner position of the building highlights its grandeur with its striking copper dome and clocktower. The Dome offers excellent stylish self-catering accommodation with stunning sea views. No expense has been spared equipping these studios and apartments with designer furniture and prominent New Zealand artwork. Available are the Dome Studios that sleep 2, the Cape & Pacific View which sleep 4, the Deco Decant & Pacific View that sleep 6, the Pacific Grand catering for 10 and the rightfully named Dome Grand that accommodates 20 guests and is spread over two floors.

Quest Napier
176 Dickens St, Napier, 4110 NZ

This historic building offers 41 serviced apartments in various combinations of studios and one and two bedroomed accommodation. The facilities are particularly good including kitchenettes, and optional breakfast. Napier is a small City, and this property is located in the nucleus near to all the major attractions.

Base Backpackers
21–23 Cambridge Terrace, Wellington, 6011 NZ
1930 John Mair

Formerly this building housed the Wellington East Post Office on the ground floor and the Post and Telegraph's Radio Section on the remaining floors. Built with a large base, stepped shaft, and recessed wings, making this an imposing building. In 2003 the upper stories were added, when the building was converted into a backpackers' hotel.

Hotel Waterloo & Backpackers
1 Bunny St, Pipitea, Wellington, 6011 NZ

This impressive hotel and backpacker's accommodation offers guest rooms to suit every budget and combination; single, twin, double with either private or shared facilities. It has various dormitories catering for larger and smaller groups and includes an all-female dorm with en-suite.

St George Accommodation
124 Willis St, Te Aro, Wellington 6011 NZ
1930 William Prouse

In 1929 the existing property on the site was bought by Grand Central Buildings Ltd., who promptly demolished the old hotel and erected a new fashionable statement piece to showcase the style of the time and it opened to much pomp and acclaim. Famous guests even included the Beatles who stayed here in 1964.

The building's main facades have various facets including podiums, bays and recessed balconies, and ingenious use of decorative mouldings which give the building a more vertical feel. It has simple single or double guest rooms with either en-suite or shared facilities and it is excellent value for money. The downside if you can call it that, is you must stay here for a minimum of one month, however, it is a great base to tour the Island. When I visited - a branch of the Wellington Dentist NZ was located ground floor!!

OUT & ABOUT
NORTH ISLAND

Victoria Theatre Trust
148-56 Victoria Rd, Devonport, Auckland, 0624 NZ
1929 John Leon Benwell

This building started life in 1912 and was a purpose-built silent movie theatre and is the earliest built cinema still in existence in the Southern Hemisphere. It was sold in 1914 and it was in 1929 that the new owner Fuller-Haywards updated it into the Art Deco cinema that we see today to accommodate the talkies. After its rise and fall and change of ownership over the decades the Victoria Theatre Trust have fortunately secured a lease to re-open the Victoria as a cinema and performance venue. They campaigned tirelessly to save this national treasure from property developers and now plan on restoring it fully with its original features.

Civic Theatre Building
267 Queen Street, Auckland, 1010 NZ
1929 Charles Bohringer

Located on the corner of Queen Street and Wellesley Street and incredibly built in just eight months the Civic opened on 20th December 1929 and was originally a 'talkie' picture house.

The theatre was equipped with a Wurlitzer 3 Manual/16 Ranks organ and continued to show films solely until 1998. It is now a vibrant theatre.

Gifford's Building
4 Vulcan Lane, Auckland, 5010 NZ/*1929 M.K. Draffin*

Designed for Alfred Gifford in 1929, this building uses its corner position as a design feature. The corner is splayed and accentuated as a vertical bay with strong horizontal lines down both facades. On the wall above the entrance lobby there is a frieze of sculptured plaster in pastel shades and the brass doors of the lift are embellished with the initials GB.

ACG Senior College Building
66 Lorne Street, Auckland, 1010 NZ
1930

This charming building, featuring polychromatic patterns and highly textured brickwork, currently houses ACG Senior College, having previously been home to the Housing Corporation and Housing New Zealand. In the past the building has also belonged to the Grand Lodge of Free Masons New Zealand.

Smith & Caughey
253-261 Queen Street, Auckland, 1010 NZ
1929 Roy Alstan Lippincott

Established in 1880, Smith & Caughey's is Auckland's oldest department store. Today the store stocks luxury brands and high-quality products spanning several departments including fashion, fragrance, cosmetics, accessories, homewares and food.

A meander around Auckland will reveal interesting architecture on every street corner including this International Style building part of a shopping area that resembles a ship complete with porthole windows. It is located just a five-minute walk from the Civic Theatre.

Landmark House
187 Queen Street, Auckland, 1010 NZ
1929 Bartley & Wade

This building is one of the few examples of commercial skyscraper architecture in New Zealand, where narrow windows and piers are used to emphasise the building's height.

The building also included a corner tower with a beacon that was lit at night. The nine-level tower building formally housed the Auckland Electricity Power Board's HQ.

It has been extensively refurbished and seismically strengthened to adhere to safety regulations.

Devonport Post Office
10 Victoria Road, Devonport, Auckland, 0000 NZ
1938 Norman Wade

The former post office at Devonport is a reinforced concrete building of Streamline Moderne design. Construction started in February of 1938 and took roughly eight months to complete at a cost £15,000. a substantial amount for the time. It retains it kudos in Devonport as an iconic building of the Interwar period.

Barton & Ross
127 Victoria Street, Hamilton 3204 NZ
c1905

This building was originally the Argus and then later became the Waikato Times. Additions to the building took place in 1928 and included an identical façade to represent a unified frontage. The original Argus building was left of the centrepiece the additional section to the right, was added for Barton & Ross.

The Local Tap House
346b Victoria Street, Hamilton, 3204 NZ
1901 John Campbell

This building with its impressive façade belonged to the former Post Office of Hamilton, hence its grand scale. It has since been modified on the ground level to accommodate the Local Tap House Restaurant/Pub.

Waiapu Cathedral of Saint John the Evangelist
28 Browning St, Napier, 4110 NZ
1965 R.S.D. Harman of Messrs Malcolm & Sweet

Following the destruction of the previous Cathedral a temporary structure stood on the site from 1931 until 1960. This Art Deco Modernist masterpiece was initially started by the Christchurch architect R.S.D. Harman, however, his untimely death meant that Kingwell Malcolm was responsible for most of the design and the building took ten years to complete from 1955-65. Its scale and beauty can only truly be appreciated by visiting it in person and the highly acclaimed heavenly voices of the choristers make visiting a service even more rewarding in this remarkable consecrated building.

Munster Chambers

61 Tennyson St, Napier South, Napier, 4110 NZ
1933 J.A. Louis Hay & Natusch and Sons

This small striking building by the great Louis Hay is both visually pleasing on the outside as it is on the inside. It is a private business and only on special occasions opens to the public.

Soundshell Stage and Forecourt
Main Parade, Napier, 4110 NZ
1935 J.T. Watson

The iconic Hollywood inspired Soundshell Stage, surrounding Colonnade and Four Arches are a showstopping statement by the local Napier architect of how the town was reinventing itself following the devastating Earthquake. Events are regularly held here throughout the year and it is free to hire for non-profit organisations.

Australian Mutual Provident Society
17 Browning St, Napier South, 4110 NZ
1934 J.A. Louis Hay

The AMP building also designed by Louis Hay has a fusion of styles in place as Hay greatly admired the Chicago School and Frank Lloyd Wright's Prairie Style. We can also see some similarities with his design of the Tobacco Co. Building with the arch doorway entrance.

Interestingly during the Second World War the upper floor was occupied by the Army and following the war it was occupied by the Rehabilitation Department. Fortunately, this Heritage Listed building has retained its original interior with large safe doors, impressive bronze grilles on the counters and authentic lighting, it is now home to the New Zealand Wine Centre.

Halsbury Chambers
74 Tennyson St, Napier, 4110 NZ
1932 J.A. Louis Hay

Proudly displaying its date and name this single storey building originally cost £1,460 to construct in 1932. It operates as a business premises and like many of the buildings in Napier it is Heritage Listed.

St Pauls Hall / Asher Hall
Tennyson St, Napier 4110, NZ

This 1930s hall now known as Asher Hall (formerly St Paul's Hall) was built on the foundations of the former Church that was partially destroyed in the earthquake and the ensuing fire that followed. It has year-round events and is fully equipped with a stage. The entrance to Tiffen Park is located on the left-hand side a few metres from the main Hall.

Napier Municipal Theatre
119 Tennyson St, Napier, 4110 NZ
1938 J.T. Watson

With a seating capacity of 993 and an impressive Pan Pac foyer that can hold up to 300 people this is an extraordinary venue. It was built from 1937-38 by the Borough architect J.T. Watson replacing the original theatre that was destroyed in the 1931 earthquake. During its 1990s refurbishment attention to detail was top priority with reproducing the original carpet design and preserving the original features and authenticity of this highly prized theatre.

Be prepared to be dazzled and delighted by the decorative features, light fittings and furnishings, tours are available and highly recommended, also be sure to book an evening event and bag a seat on the front row the acoustics and atmosphere during performances is second to none.

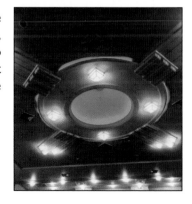

National Tobacco Company Building
1 Ossian St, Ahuriri, Napier, 4110 NZ
1933 J.A. Louis Hay

This is one of the most famous buildings in Napier for its ornate design that strides between Art Nouveau and Art Deco. It incorporates both geometrics and naturalistic iconography. The stucco decoration around the door of bull-rushes and roses were sculpted by hand and fruit and roses are themed throughout the building.

No expense was spared on the building and the wooden doors alone cost £600 which during the depression years was an extortionate amount. From 1954 to 2001 it was known as the Rothmans Building and the exterior was painted in their trademark blue, however, in 1996 it was restored to its original colour scheme of terracotta and buff. The elaborate foyer includes marble, columns, leadlight windows, and domed ceiling. It is located an 8-minute drive from the centre of Napier and tours can be booked in advance.

Charleston Chic

Shop 1 Upper Tennyson St, Masonic Hotel Building, Napier, 4110 NZ

Whether you have planned your trip to Napier to coincide with the summer or winter Art Deco Festivals, it is *de rigueur* to dress the part. Whatever your budget or taste a visit to Charleston Chic is a must! The knowledgeable and helpful shop owner can find the right outfit and accessories to suit anyone and has a vast array of original and quality reproduction items. The shop is easy to find as it is adjoined to the iconic Masonic Hotel building.

Art Deco Trust

7 Tennyson St, Napier South, 2110 NZ

No trip to Napier would be complete until the Art Deco Trust has been visited. This really should be the first port of call as they have boundless information about the surroundings and offer cultural events including walks around the historic Art Deco Heritage buildings.

Even the sightseeing tour bus is streamline!

Daily Telegraph Building
49 Tennyson St, Napier, 4110 NZ
1932 E.A. Williams

Here we have an exceedingly appealing building by the prolific architect Ernest Arthur Williams whose practice included eight architectural draughtsmen to assist with the large amount of commissions following the earthquake. The Daily

Telegraph building operated up until 1999 printing newspapers. Noteworthy features include the lotus topped columns, zigzags and symmetry of the building. The interior is accessible and has been restored with the original chandelier's and flooring.

ASB Bank
Corner of Hastings and Emerson St, Napier, 4110 NZ
1932-33 Crichton, McKay & Haughton

This is arguably the best example of Maori motifs incorporated in a building in Napier. The architecture is defined as a Stripped Classical Art Deco building. The exterior cement plaster work is in subtle subdued colours incorporating key Maori designs and according to the apprentice plasterer (the late Doug Dalton) 12 or 14 plasterers worked for a month or more on the decorative features. The striking interior with traditional red, white and black Maori designs feature on the ceiling and the main

pattern is known as Kowhaiwhai, look for the bronze grille over the high window as this incorporates the shape of *Rumano the whale* as do the iron gates. The building is Heritage Listed and has changed hands on several occasions; however, it is still operating as a bank and can freely be entered and admired.

Hawkes Bay Museum & Art Gallery
1 Tennyson St, Napier, 4110 NZ
1936 J.A. Louis Hay

Born out of the Hawke's Bay Philosophical Society this building by Chief Architect Louis Hay was housed to display the 1931 earthquake artefacts. Over the decades it has had several name changes and it is now incorporated into the 2013 contemporary Art Gallery and is known as MTG Hawke's Bay.

Whichever way you turn and on every street corner in Napier you will be surrounded by an abundance of rich architecture showcasing arguably the best of low storey Art Deco buildings to be found in one concentration in the world.

Drain covers are Art Deco in design and even a statement streetlight.

Spirit of Napier – Statue located along the parade.

The **Tom Parker Fountain** located along the promenade in Napier is enjoyed by all both day and night when it is illuminated. It was inaugurated the night before Christmas Eve in 1936 and was a gift from a generous local shop owner Tom Parker who donated one thousand pounds for the local architect J.T. Watson to design. Parker frequently visited England and was so impressed with the illuminated fountain in Bournemouth he decided that Napier needed one to bring cheer and joy to the people following the long years of the depression. This it certainly did as the visual feast of the modern lighting was much coveted by Napier residents and visitors and it still is today.

Head a short walk from the centre of Napier to the Clive Square bus terminus and you will be in for a treat. The exuberant life-size wall art on the local conveniences is vibrant and fun and expertly painted.

On **Marine Parade, Napier** the 1.5m (4.9ft) bronze statue of Pania sits proudly dressed in a traditional piupiu skirt. The Maori mythology surrounding Pania of the reef was frequently relayed to the parishioners of the area by the Anglican Bishop of Aotearoa and in 1954 funds were raised to commemorate this. Following a local competition, the model was chosen and photographed, these pictures were sent to the Italian Carrera marble company who sculpted her in clay, and this was used to produce the bronze statue.

When in Napier be prepared to be fully immersed in Art Deco, this larger than life size bronze statue of an impeccable flapper and her trusty companion are a constant reminder of the era that this small City rose from.

The Streamline sightseeing bus takes passengers for tours around the city and nearby suburbs to admire the outstanding buildings and private residences that the proud owners are happy to show off.

Experience the thrill of travelling on the original 1930s train from Napier to Hastings - regular trips are available throughout the day.

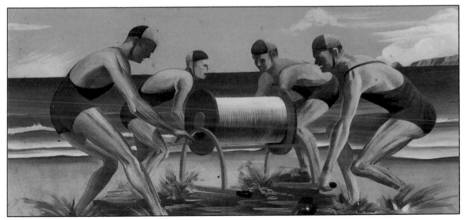

This original 1930s painting can be seen at the Yacht club along the parade.

The hustle and bustle of the Art Deco festivities, spectators enjoying a picnic and concert from the Shell Bandstand (out of sight) with the Dome building in the background.

HASTINGS

The town of Hastings is easily accessible being in the heart of Hawkes Bay less than a twenty-minute drive from Napier. It has an abundance of Art Deco buildings and shop facades to tantalise and delight visitors. The modernist designed street lighting compliments the buildings in this area of outstanding natural and man-made beauty.

Focal Point Cinema & Café
126 Heretaunga St East, Hastings, 4122 NZ

This two-screen cinema and café is housed in the 1933-34 former State Theatre building designed by architect J.T. Watson. It reopened in 2014 following major refurbishment and offers luxurious environs with 1920s décor.

Unfortunately, little to none of the original interior exists and the exterior was extended both outwards and upwards in 1994, however, it has been pleasingly kept in the Art Deco style.

Palmerston Ladies Conveniences
The Square, Palmerston North, 4410 NZ

Palmerston can certainly boost that they have the some of the best public toilets in the Southern Hemisphere.

The conveniences were built in 1936 and they certainly make an impact proving that no expense was spared in the design of

these necessities. They come complete with showers for a small fee and changing facilities along with a dedicated on-site attendant.

Square Edge Community Arts Centre
47 The Square, Palmerston North, 4410 NZ

This building can be described as the hub of the community as it showcases the local artistic talent, has venues and spaces to hire along with marvellous ethical food and coffee at the Café Royale within. The building is highly impressive dominating the area with its splendorous design. Originally the building opened in 1892 as the Colonial Bank of New Zealand, it underwent several ownerships and additions, and it was in 1945 that Reginald Thorrold Jaggard upgraded and designed the Art Deco façade.

ANZ Bank
1 Grey Street, Tauranga, 3110 NZ
1938 Edgecombe & White

This building was originally the first purpose-built Post Office in Tauranga. Its construction signified the increasing needs of Tauranga, which developed rapidly during the 1920s and 1930s and it was opened on 1st December 1938. It is an important example of the work of architects Edgecombe and White of Hamilton who designed several other significant public buildings. I also quite admire the scalloped mosaic crossroads at the intersection so check these out on your Art Deco travels.

James Smith Building
Cuba and Manners St, Wellington, 6011 NZ
1932 King & Dawson

James Smith the famous Wellington retailer bought the building in 1866 but it was not until 1932 that it was given its Art Deco appearance. Further down Manners Street is a 1934 addition to the building, designed by the same architects.

Korn Ferry Business Consultants
5 Cable St, Wellington, 6011 NZ
1932 William Turnbull

Formerly the Wellington Free Ambulance building the architect Turnbull maximised his efforts to give all four elevations architectural interest - largely hidden for much of its existence, however, this appealing building has been admired by many for this reason.

City Art Gallery
Civic Centre, Wellington 6011
1939 Gummer & Ford with Messenger Taylor & Wolfe

Originally the Wellington City Library, this stylish Stripped Classical building, was completed in 1939. In 1990–2 a new Public Library was built on Victoria Street and its predecessor was successfully converted into the City Art Gallery.

ACCOMMODATION
SOUTH ISLAND

New City Hotel
527 Colombo St, Christchurch, 8011 NZ
1930 Guthrie & Williamson

Located on the corner of Colombo and Bath Streets, the building has three storeys above ground and a basement level.

The Streamline Moderne building is constructed of reinforced concrete, and features include the rounded north-east corner, unadorned planar facades, horizontal orientation, and large steel casement windows. Several of the original fixtures still exist including the main staircase, timber panelling and room service buttons.

Law Courts Hotel
53-65 Stuart Street, Dunedin 9016, NZ
1937

Located in a prime location this hotel having originally been founded as the Auld Scotland Hotel in 1863 was rebuilt in its current style in 1937 and refurbished for the Queen's visit in 1954. It is a relaxed and comfortable hotel with the casual Magic Moments

Restaurant. Particularly nice are the large double rooms accommodated in the curvilinear part of the building with an expanse of windows. In total the hotel has 14 double guest rooms, 4 single and 5 twin rooms all with private facilities.

OUT & ABOUT

Alice Cinema & Film Specialists
209 Tuam St, Christchurch Central, Christchurch, 0811 NZ
1932 John Mair

This quirky boutique cinema located in the former Post Office building on Tuam Street. The cinema has two themed screens featuring a Wonderland and an Egyptian Revival style of décor. It has a café/bar and a retail outlet for film buffs. Well worth a visit for its originality and concept. Fortunately, the Stripped Classical style building was not badly damaged in the 2011 earthquake and has now been fully restored.

Christchurch Tramway
109 Worcester St, Christchurch Central, Christchurch, 8011 NZ

The tram service in Christchurch is a fine way to get around the main routes of the town.

Especially nice is an afternoon or evening meal in the special dining carriage with a 1930s style interior.

Light and window features at the Tramway central station.

New Regent Street

New Regent Street Precinct, Christchurch, 8011 NZ
1932 H. Francis Willis

This pedestrian precinct in Christchurch, is one of the city's major tourist attractions. The buildings in the streets are listed as Category One by Heritage New Zealand, and in addition, the entire street has a Historic Area Listing. During the depression it was described as New Zealand's most beautiful street.

It has brought pleasure and hope to shoppers and tourists with its uplifting abundance of colour and design. The buildings feature shaped gables, medallions, tiled window hoods, and barley-twist columns as well as beautiful pastel coloured facades. The Spanish Mission style fused with Stripped Classical and Interwar Modern all enrich its character and appeal.

Rydal House

29 Grey Street, Tauranga, 3110 NZ
1955 Stanley Fearn

This building demonstrates a change in architectural design in New Zealand.

The external appearance now looked Modernist and detailing was restrained and minimal with little embellishment. The three-storey building is private commercial premises.

Central Fire Station

2–38 Oriental Parade, Oriental Bay, Wellington, 6011 NZ
1937 C.H. Mitchell

This impressive building was planned on two levels with the main station on Oriental Parade and the accommodation to the rear, it is imposing in scale with a symmetrical façade and clock tower. The clock originally belonged to the town hall and dates to 1922, it was donated to the Fire Station in 1932.

National War Memorial
Taranaki St/Old Buckle St, Mount Cook, Wellington, 6011 NZ
1931–32 Gummer & Ford

This moving memorial is positioned that it can be visible from all of the city including ships that enter the harbour. If consists of steps, a pool, forecourt, and a bell tower, and at the base it houses the Hall of Memories. The building was officially dedicated at the 1932 ANZAC Day ceremonies, but it was not until 1964 that the Hall of Memories was finally completed.

Carly Harris Designs
154–156 Cuba St, Wellington, 6011 NZ
1935 James Bennie

This Heritage Listed building has prominent Art Deco features with a show stopping sunburst motif between the second storey and parapet and a series of vertical mouldings. It was originally planned as a private hotel called *York House* and it was renamed *The Vic* in 1951. It has undergone different ownerships over the decades and is now a high-end retail boutique.

State Insurance Building
116 Worcester St, Christchurch, 8011 NZ
1935 Cecil W Wood

The State Insurance Building is a fine example of an architect choosing to utilise Māori imagery. Before the earthquakes, this building was home to the Design and Arts College of New Zealand as well as the Kaplan International English School. To the casual observer the building looks comparatively plain but on closer inspection a lot of decoration is visible most of which is traditional Māori carving. The building was severely damaged in the 2011 earthquake and unoccupied, the owners sold it to an engineering company in 2018 who are fully restoring this Heritage Listed building.

Robert McDougall Art Gallery
9 Rolleston Avenue, Christchurch, 8013 NZ
1932 Edward Armstrong

This single-storey building located in the Botanic Gardens is constructed of brick and concrete and faced with Oamaru stone and the gallery has a large central hall, with scagliola columns and marble floors. A unique feature and of great importance are the skylights that allow natural light to fall onto the displayed artworks without the light falling onto the visitors or the floors. Unfortunately, since the new Art Gallery opened in 2002 this building has become redundant apart from the occasional exhibitions that took place up until 2010. The building requires an extensive renovation and restoration program to make it earthquake worthy, and this is estimated to be in the region of $37 million. The building is Council owned and is the legacy of the McDougall Industrialists who made their money from biscuits.

West Avon Apartments
Corner of Montreal Street & Hereford Street, Christchurch, 8013 NZ
c1936 W. M. Lawry

These extremely desirable Streamlined Moderne apartments are constructed with reinforced concrete strip footings under the perimeter and internal load bearing walls.

The symmetrical façade has bold decorative vertical and horizontal lines and steel framed casement windows. The flat roof appearance is due to the raised parapet. In its day, this ultra-modern building included apartments with pre-installed fixtures and fittings, including built-in furniture.

New Zealand Railways Road Services Building
35 Queens Gardens, Dunedin, 9016 NZ
1936 E.Miller

This bold curvilinear plastered building is designed with striking vertical speed lines at its entrance. It is one of the most important Art Deco buildings of its period and was constructed at a time when few large buildings were being erected in Dunedin. The building is now the Toitu - Otago Settlers Museum.

Angus Motors Ltd Building
471 Princes Street, Dunedin.
1938

Parts of the Edwardian brick masonry building dated back to before 1882. Its Art Deco facade was added in 1938, followed by a glass facade in 1987. Now trading as Toffs Second-hand Clothing.

Order of St John Building
17 York Place, Dunedin 9016, NZ
1938 James Hodge White

The Order of St John had new premises in York Place built in 1938 to mark the golden jubilee of first-aid activity in Dunedin. The symmetrical composition and decorative plasterwork, which is enriched by a genial colour scheme, make this building one of the finest examples of Art Deco architecture in Dunedin.

© Portfolio Amalgamated Builders Limited

Rialto Cinema
11 Moray Place, Dunedin, 9016 NZ
1936 Edmond Anscombe

This powerful and memorable cinema was acquired by the Australian Showman Thomas O'Brien in 1928, after first opening as the 2,000-seat Empire Theatre in 1916. Designed in a Moorish Atmospheric style, with starred ceiling, minarets, and a Taj Mahal-like proscenium the theatre could also boast of having a Christie 2 Manual/10 Ranks theatre organ.

Art Deco Societies

Australia

Art Deco and Modernism Society of Australia Inc.
Robin Grow – President
artdeco.org.au

Art Deco in the Tropics, Innisfail, Australia
artdeco-innisfail.com

Twentieth Century Heritage Society of NSW & ACT, Australia
twentieth.org.au

Beaumaris Modern
beaumarismodern.com.au

New Zealand

Art Deco Trust, Napier, New Zealand
artdeconapier.com

Club Moderne, Auckland, New Zealand
clubmoderne.org.nz

Please note that this is not an exhaustive list as new Societies are formed and various regions have a presence via social media and Facebook pages dedicated to Art Deco.

GLOSSARY

Arts & Crafts - This social and artistic movement was active the latter part of the 19th century. Among its main proponents were William Morris, John Ruskin and Walter Crane. Charles Rennie Macintosh, who was an exponent of the Glasgow School. It came about as a reaction to industrialisation and mass-produced goods. The idle was to produce bespoke handcrafted items for the masses, however this was not feasible due to the intensive hours of labour and production costs. This meant only the richer people could afford the items, which was in complete juxtaposition to the mandate of the movement.

Art Nouveau - This style of arts and design was popular c.1890-1910 and is recognisable with its references to nature and organic sinuous designs. Often these designs would include a female form with long flowing hair. The style transferred to jewellery, glass ware, illustration and architecture. Amongst the main proponents of the time were: Aubrey Beardsley, Louis Comfort Tiffany, Antoni Gaudi, Max Beckmann and Alphonse Mucha.

Curvilinear - Design in a building consisting of curved flowing lines, employed in Streamline Moderne buildings.

Functionalism - This architectural and design style made popular by the Bauhaus advocated that buildings should be designed based solely on the purpose and function of the building. It opposed unnecessary adornments and decoration to the building.

Interwar Style – The term applied to the new modernist architectural style in Australia and New Zealand between the First and Second World Wars.

Marquee - A roof like structure, often bearing a signboard, projecting over an entrance, of a theatre or hotel.

Oculus - A circular window (porthole) which is a familiar feature in Art Deco buildings especially when a reference to the sea or ocean liners is predominant in the architecture.

Parallelepiped - This is a three-dimensional building, formed by six parallelograms.

Streamline Moderne - Emerged in the 1930s. Its architectural style emphasised curving forms, long horizontal lines and sometimes nautical elements. As seen in ocean liner designed buildings and some lidos. It resonated the times of technological advancement and is associated with the innovations of high-speed motors cars and aeroplanes.

Vernacular - An architectural style that is designed based on the local needs and the availability of construction materials, reflecting and incorporating local traditions.

Saving our Art Deco Heritage

Having travelled extensively over the years for business and pleasure, I have felt privileged and honoured to have; slept in, dined at, drank in, swam in, and laughed in, some of our most phenomenal twentieth century architecture. To have sat in the most exquisite Art Deco furniture and experienced the best in design; Art Deco touches every nuance of our lives. No architectural movement or style has had such an effect on so many people and objects Worldwide. It is unique - and that is why we must protect, preserve, and restore our Twentieth Century Art Deco Heritage for future generations to enjoy.

I am always saddened to hear that a place I once visited has been demolished to make way for a new development or that is it was unviable despite local outcry. However, I am euphoric when I hear that a *Peoples Trust* or *Community Project* has been formed to raise the profile of a building and ultimately restore it back to its former glory.

I urge everyone who has a passion for Art Deco to seek out your nearest monument whether that be a cinema, restaurant, pub, lido etc., and support it. It is no good just to save these iconic buildings, they need to be continually utilised and championed to keep them viable.

My hat goes off (and I have many) to all you dedicated and hardworking people who often go unrecognised in your campaigning and fundraising efforts. We owe you our sincere thanks in highlighting and helping to save our iconic Art Deco Heritage.

Lastly but certainly not least, my wholehearted gratitude goes out to the Art Deco Societies' in Australia and New Zealand and around the World for championing, celebrating, highlighting and protecting our Art Deco Heritage.

Thank You!

Credits & Acknowledgements

Where to start, it must be with my Editor, Elizabeth, her endless hours of devoted time and patience making sense of my scribblings and 4am messages, I applaud you. To all my family, friends and colleagues, who have endlessly supported me in all my ventures and rallied me on when needed I thank you. John Nicholson and his book 'Building Sydney Harbour Bridge (ISBN 1865082597) which travelled with me and crossed the Bridge! To Passepartout my rock. Paul at Melita Press and Chris Lloyd my Agent, I could not do it without you guys, cheers.

My sincere thanks to the Hotels, Restaurants, Cinemas, Theatres and Tourist Boards who have kindly allowed me to use photographs and supplied me with additional information. To all the Art Deco Societies throughout the World who are not only my kindred spirits, but are helping to preserve, educate and entertain future generations, about our Art Deco Heritage.

Finally, I would like to acknowledge all the passing acquaintances, friends and associates that I have made during my lifetime of travels and lectures. I feel enriched and honoured to have spent time in your company and country.

During the compilation of this book the author and publisher have made every effort to ensure that the information in this book was correct at the time of going to press. The author and publisher do not assume and hereby disclaim any liability to any part for any loss, damage, or disruption caused by errors or omissions, whether such errors or omissions result from negligence, accident or any other cause.

Any further information can be obtained at www.artdeco-traveller.co.uk

INDEX

INDEX

INDEX

INDEX